Orchid Care for Beginners

A Comprehensive Guide to Thriving Orchids with Easy Care Tips, Proven Techniques, and Expert Secrets for Stunning, Long-Lasting Blooms

© **Copyright 2025 - All rights reserved.**

The content contained within this book may not be reproduced, duplicated, or transmitted without direct written permission from the author or the publisher.

Under no circumstances will any blame or legal responsibility be held against the publisher or author for any damages, reparation, or monetary loss due to the information contained within this book, either directly or indirectly.

Legal Notice:

This book is copyright-protected. It is only for personal use. You cannot amend, distribute, sell, use, quote, or paraphrase any part of the content within this book without the consent of the author or publisher.

Disclaimer Notice:

Please note the information contained within this document is for educational and entertainment purposes only. All effort has been executed to present accurate, up-to-date, reliable, and complete information. No warranties of any kind are declared or implied. Readers acknowledge that the author is not engaging in the rendering of legal, financial, medical, or professional advice. The content within this book has been derived from various sources. Please consult a licensed professional before attempting any techniques outlined in this book.

By reading this document, the reader agrees that under no circumstances is the author responsible for any losses, direct or indirect, that are incurred as a result of the use of the information contained within this document, including, but not limited to, errors, omissions, or inaccuracies.

Table of Contents

Introduction 1

Chapter 1: Understanding Orchids – The Basics 3

Chapter 2: Choosing the Right Orchid for You 11

Chapter 3: Potting and Repotting Orchids 28

**Chapter 4: Watering and Humidity –
The Most Common Orchid Issue** 36

**Chapter 5: Light and Temperature –
Creating the Ideal Growing Environment** 47

Chapter 6: Fertilizing and Feeding Orchids 56

**Chapter 7: Common Orchid Problems
and How to Fix Them** 65

**Chapter 8: Orchid Propagation –
Growing More Orchids from One** 80

**Chapter 9: Encouraging More Blooms
and Longer-Lasting Flowers** 85

**Chapter 10: Creative Orchid Display
and Styling Ideas** 94

**Chapter 11: Advanced Orchid Care
and Expert Tips** 103

**Chapter 12: Final Takeaways and
Orchid Success Tips** 114

Conclusion 120

References 123

Introduction

Orchids are beautiful flowers that enhance your home's decor and add a beautiful scent. Growing plants can do wonders for your mental health, reducing stress, connecting you with nature, and improving your mood. Watching your flowers grow also gives you a sense of accomplishment.

The book begins by exploring the history and popularity of orchids. It explains their anatomy, growth cycle, and the difference between epiphytic and terrestrial orchids and also debunks most common myths about orchid care.

Some orchids are easy to grow, while others can be challenging. You will learn about the best orchid species for beginners and experienced growers so you can choose the right one for you.

Going to a store and purchasing an orchid isn't always easy. You need to choose a healthy plant that will grow into a strong flower, and it's essential to recognize the difference between a healthy and an unhealthy one.

Choosing the right pot for your plant's needs is important. The book explains the difference between clay, plastic pots, and hanging baskets. It also explores the best orchid potting mediums, their uses, when and how to repot orchids, and tips to avoid repotting shock.

Many new plant owners overwater or underwater their orchids, causing root rot or dryness. Understanding the right watering techniques will prolong your flower's life.

You will also understand light requirements for different orchid types, the best indoor light setups, and how temperature changes impact orchids.

Plants thrive when they are well-fertilized. However, with so many fertilizers available, you may struggle to find the right one for your orchid. This book covers the necessary information for your plants' nutritional needs.

While growing orchids is easy, you may still face some issues. Understanding the most common problems growers face and their solutions, such as yellowing leaves, falling buds, dehydration, rotten roots, pest control issues, and orchid diseases, will keep your plant healthy and thriving.

Now that your flowers have grown and bloomed, you can use them to decorate your home. The book offers tips on making stunning orchid displays and different arrangements to add a personal touch to your surroundings. It also includes expert tips for growing rare orchids and specialty species, orchid care hacks that save time and money, and unconventional orchid care methods.

This book is perfect for beginners because it is easy to understand and includes simple, detailed, and easy-to-follow instructions.

Begin your journey with orchids and learn everything about growing these gorgeous flowers.

Chapter 1: Understanding Orchids – The Basics

Who doesn't love orchids? They are beautiful and captivating with unique colors, shapes, and mesmerizing fragrances, almost making you believe they come from an enchanting world. These flowers have a calming effect and can reduce stress, making them the perfect addition to your home. Orchids also symbolize charm, beauty, and love, making them the perfect gift for many occasions.

1. Orchids symbolize charm, beauty and love. Source: https://unsplash.com/photos/purple-moth-orchids-in-bloom-ywEfzLduYB4

This chapter explores the history of orchids, their popularity, anatomy, and growth cycle. It also explains the difference between epiphytic and terrestrial orchids and debunks common myths about orchid care.

Orchid History and Popularity

Orchids have a long and rich history that dates back around 120 million years, making them one of the oldest flowers in the world. There are 28,000 species, all belonging to the Orchidaceae family. Although scientists and historians agree that these flowers may be millions of years old, their recorded history is believed to have begun in Japan and China around 4000 years ago. Ancient civilizations used them for medicinal purposes, such as treating infections, wounds, fever, and coughs.

Over time, their popularity spread to other countries thanks to their stunning fragrance and beauty. The world began to admire these beautiful flowers and attach many meanings to them. They were symbols of nobility, refinement, and elegance in ancient Japan and China while they represented fertility, spirituality, and love in Indonesia, Thailand, and India.

In ancient Greece, the flowers were associated with virility and had various uses, from cooking to determining a child's gender. They were also popular in Victorian England and featured in Roman art, representing prosperity, rebirth, and celebration. The orchid fascinated many scientists, such as Charles Darwin, who wrote a book called "Fertilisation of Orchids," while Confucius also found the flowers fascinating and admired their scent.

Orchids are no ordinary flowers. Over the years, they have become cultural symbols that people worldwide connect with and admire.

Orchid Anatomy 101

2. The orchid consists of four parts: the leaves, roots, stems, and flowers. Source: https://unsplash.com/photos/three-pink-flowers-NcVUlN_uImU

Leaves

All plants have leaves, and the orchids are no different. Leaves are used during the photosynthesis process to convert light into energy. Their shapes differ from one orchid species to another. For instance, the Oncidium and Dendrobium Nobile orchids have flexible, thin leaves, while the Phalaenopsis orchids have tough, rigid, and dark green ones with a shade of purple at the end.

Roots

While orchid roots may look different depending on the flower's type, they all have the same functions. They are usually very thin, like hair, and coated with velamen. The Phalaenopsis orchid's roots are covered with fleshy and thick velamen, while the Oncidium orchid's root coat is white and very thin instead of the common green/grey color. Roots connect the orchid to the tree or soil to help absorb water.

Some orchid species have aerial roots, such as the Phalaenopsis orchid. These are unique roots that wander off and grow away from the potting medium, and they support the orchid's main roots. For example, if the roots get damaged and can't absorb the water, the aerial roots take over to absorb the nutrients.

Stems

Sarcochilus, Vanda, Phalaenopsis, and other orchids that grow upwards have stems. However, other types grow linearly and look similar to each other. They are connected by rhizomes and produce their own flowers, leaves, and roots.

Flowers

Under the right light conditions, many types of orchids produce flower spikes, while the Dendrobium Nobile orchids produce flowers from the cane. Some flower spikes grow very fast, like the Phalaenopsis orchids, while others, like the Oncidium orchids, take a long time to develop.

The Orchid's Growth Cycle

Orchids go through six stages, and you need to learn about them to know your flower's needs during each one.

Seed Germination

This is the first stage in an orchid's growth cycle. The seedlings grow and develop during this time, which can last a few weeks or months. It is also called the "Keiki development." Keiki means "baby" in Hawaiian, which refers to the stage when the orchid looks like a small version of its adult self. It keeps growing until it matures and blooms.

3. *Keiki development, seed germination process. Source: https://upload.wikimedia.org/wikipedia/commons/thumb/b/b7/Phalaenopsis_keiki_growth_progression.jpg/1280px-Phalaenopsis_keiki_growth_progression.jpg*

Root Growth

This stage occurs under the soil, where the root system produces new growths. Those are called pseudobulbs and can grow to eight inches tall. Long and thin leaves grow from the pseudobulbs and absorb nutrients and water from the plant.

Leaf Production

An orchid can take a year to produce a leaf. Depending on the type of orchid, it can take the leaf between four to eight months to fully grow. The leaves start to emerge from the stems' tips once the plant grows taller. They remain attached to the flower for the rest of its life cycle.

Flower Spikes

Flower spikes grow after the leaves mature, which can take three months or more, depending on the orchid's species. Soon after, the flowers begin to grow.

Blooming

Orchids bloom three months after the flower spike grows. They produce large flowers during this stage, lasting weeks or months, depending on the orchid's species.

Dormancy

Blooming requires a lot of energy, which can slow down or stop the orchid's growth, which occurs during the dormancy stage. The leaves turn yellow and fall off, making people believe their plants are dying. However, this isn't true. This is a normal and significant stage in the orchid's cycle. It allows it to rejuvenate and rest to continue blooming and growing.

Epiphytic vs. Terrestrial Orchids

4. *Epiphytic Orchid. Source: https://upload.wikimedia.org/wikipedia/commons/3/30/Epiphytic_Orchid_%28Bulbophyllum_pulchellum%29_%2823033427699%29.jpg*

Epiphytic orchids have succulent leaves with sunken stomata, cuticles, and thick cell walls, while terrestrial orchids have tubers, corms, or rhizomes. Terrestrial plants absorb nutrients through their roots from the soil, while epiphytic plants grow on trees and get their nutrients from decayed plant parts on the surface.

5. *The bearded grass pink orchid is a terrestrial orchid. Source: https://commons.wikimedia.org/wiki/File:Bearded_Grass_Pink_Orchid_(5433321237).jpg*

Debunking Common Orchid Care Myths

Myth: Orchids Need Lots of Sunlight

Fact: Direct sunlight can damage the flower. Most orchid species thrive in indirect light.

Myth: Orchids Should Be Watered Once a Week

Fact: Orchids should be watered when their potting mix gets dry.

Myth: Orchids Require Expensive Fertilizers

Fact: You can use any type of fertilizer.

Myth: Orchids Bloom Once a Year

Fact: Many orchid species bloom several times a year.

Myth: Orchids Should be Frequently Repotted

Fact: Orchids should be repotted every year or two or when the roots outgrow the pot or the potting medium breaks.

Myth: You Can Only Grow Orchids Outdoors

Fact: Many orchid species thrive indoors.

Myth: Don't Touch Orchid Roots

Fact: You can touch the roots when repotting or checking the flower's health.

Orchids are beautiful plants you can easily grow at home. They don't require a garden and can thrive in an indoor environment. These flowers have a rich history, deep symbolism, and a soothing impact, making them the perfect addition to your home and a great gift for a loved one.

Chapter 2: Choosing the Right Orchid for You

This chapter offers recommendations for choosing the right orchids based on your experience level and home environment. It also has tips for picking out healthy plants in the store.

Best Orchids for Beginners

Phalaenopsis (Moth Orchid)

6. Moth orchid. Source: https://commons.wikimedia.org/wiki/File:Phalaenopsis_philippinensis_Orchi_008.jpg

Known as the most resilient orchid variety in the world, the moth orchid is the perfect choice for first-time owners. It can adapt to lower and higher light conditions and humidity levels. It prefers moderate air temperatures and isn't picky about soil. Moth orchids also flower multiple times a year, so if you get several, you'll always have at least one in bloom.

Dendrobium

7. *Dendrobium. Source: https://commons.wikimedia.org/wiki/File:Dendrobium_phalaenopsis_Kiev.jpg*

While these orchids have a broader range of requirements, none are hard to grow. They have large (sometimes hanging) and long-lasting blooms and thrive in medium to high humidity. They are adaptable and won't suffer much if moisture levels vary. They also prefer moderately warm temperatures and partial light exposure.

Oncidium (Dancing Lady Orchids)

8. *Oncidium orchids. Source: https://commons.wikimedia.org/wiki/File:Oncidium_splendidum_1001_Orchids.jpg*

Oncidium orchids are a statement piece known for their fragrant blooms that vary from vanilla to chocolate. Despite this, they aren't hard to grow, requiring moderately high daytime and low night temperatures. They thrive at moderately high humidity levels of 70-85%.

Aspasia

9. *Aspasia. Source: https://commons.wikimedia.org/wiki/File:Aspasia_silvana_003.jpg*

As one of the smallest orchids, the Aspasia is also an easy-to-grow but compelling plant due to its large starlike flowers. You can keep them on the windowsill in filtered light or in baskets in partial shade. They are adaptable if you provide them with humidity levels close to their native tropical regions (over 85%).

Brassia (Spider Orchid)

10. Brassia orange delight. Source: https://commons.wikimedia.org/wiki/File:A_and_B_Larsen_orchids_-_Brassia_Orange_Delight_DSCN0997z.jpg

If you're looking for an undemanding orchid that blooms several times a year, bringing lots of flowers each time, the spider orchid may be the perfect pick. It loves the sun, moderate to higher temperatures, and humidity above 85%. It is the most active in spring, but you can keep it in abutment bloom if you regularly spray it with water or use a humidifier.

Cattleya

11. *Cattleya. Source: https://commons.wikimedia.org/wiki/File:Cattleya_Beaumesnil_Parme_1001_Orchids.jpg*

As another miniature orchid, the Cattleya is a lover of tropical conditions. However, it's good at tolerating slight environmental changes (temperature or humidity drops). Moreover, regardless of the species you opt for, their care is the same. This makes them ideal for those wanting a collection of mini orchids in a small space.

Encyclia

12. Encyclia. Source: https://commons.wikimedia.org/wiki/File:Orchidaceae_Encyclia_ osmantha_2.jpg

The Encyclia orchids are also very attractive with their prominent branching spikes and wide flowers. Another bonus is that they are happy to grow and bloom actively in bright light, moderately moist soil, and air humidity. You won't have to worry about maintaining high humidity levels when growing these.

Orchids for More Experienced Growers

Vanilla Planifolia (Vanilla Orchid)

13. The vanilla orchid. Source: https://www.flickr.com/photos/mmmavocado/6998639597

The vanilla orchid is a true tropical species requiring day temperatures of 80-95°F and night temperatures of 60-70°F, as well as humidity levels up to 70-85%. However, since it also needs frequent air movements, it fits into the advanced growth category. To entice it to bloom and grow fruit, you must alternate between giving it filtered and indirect and bright and direct lighting.

Anguloa Uniflora (Tulip Orchid)

14. Tulip orchid. Source: https://commons.wikimedia.org/wiki/File:Anguloa_uniflora_(14775571791).jpg

Also called the swaddled baby orchid (as its flowers look like tiny babies swaddled in a blanket), the tulip orchid is in the intermediate to hard-to-grow category. Its cinnamon-scented creamy-looking blooms will last a long time, but only if kept at a daytime temperature of 60-80°F. It requires medium-intensity filtered lighting and humidity levels of 70-80%. Many grow these orchids in heated greenhouses with built-in misting systems.

Dracula Simia (Monkey Orchid)

15. *The monkey orchid. Source: https://commons.wikimedia.org/wiki/File:15.Dracula_simia,_the _Monkey_Face_Orchid_(10957423336).jpg*

The monkey orchid is perfect for those with some experience in growing orchids. To make it thrive and grow those characteristic monkey face-shaped flowers, keep it at slightly cooler daytime temperatures of 60-85°F. It also prefers low and indirect lighting and moderate to high humidity levels of 70-80%. If you keep it in these conditions, it can grace your home for up to 20 years.

Cypripedium (Lady Slipper Orchid)

16. The lady slipper orchid. Source: https://commons.wikimedia.org/wiki/File:Cypripedium_parviflorum_Orchi_014.jpg

One of the few orchid species that thrives in partial shade, the lady slipper orchid is the perfect choice for outdoor growth. It needs moist soil and moderate to high air humidity levels but prefers slightly cooler temperatures of 60-80°F. It also loves air movement and well-draining soil, so its roots won't get clogged with water.

Calopogon Tuberosus (Grass Pink Orchid)

17. The grass pink orchid. Source: https://upload.wikimedia.org/wikipedia/commons/e/e4/Calopogon_tuberosus_15-p.bot-calopo.pulche-005.jpg

The grass pink orchid, another species suited for well-aerated soil and environment, is a little more demanding. While it requires air movement, it also needs high humidity levels (above 80%), higher temperatures, and light exposure. It is also more sensitive to impurities in the water, and its roots only thrive in a regular source of clean water. Otherwise, they can become diseased and won't prosper no matter how good the lighting and temperature conditions you provide.

How to Choose Orchids Based on Your Home Environment

When choosing orchids for your home, you have to consider the environment they will live in. By picking out species that thrive in your house, you'll be able to enjoy their beauties for a long time. Below are some tips for choosing orchids based on your home environment.

Lighting Conditions

While light plays a crucial role in the growth and development of all orchids, not all species require the same amount or type of lighting. Some thrive in partial lighting, while others need much more light. By picking out species that thrive in the lighting conditions in the space you've chosen for them, you'll keep them healthy and blooming. For example, did you know some orchids can be kept in a bathroom? Many bathrooms have low lighting (and little to no natural light source), yet some species will thrive there, too. The key is to pick the ones that love higher humidity. Others will prefer well-lit places like window sills.

Humidity

Even orchids that prefer sunny places require moderate amounts of humidity. They usually don't thrive in humidity levels below 50%. Many people use humidifiers in their homes. If you do, you can keep your orchids in the same room as the humidifier. Your plants will thank you for this with luscious blooms. Alternatively, you can use a humidity tray, which only slightly raises the humidity, making it suitable for plants thriving at moderate humidity levels.

Temperature

Like high humidity, higher temperatures are preferred by some orchid species. Some prefer a temperature around 65-75°F, others will require slightly higher or lower temperatures. Originating from tropical regions, many orchids thrive on temperatures closer to their native land. These are typically the ones that also prefer plenty of light and moisture in the air. Choose species depending on the temperature of their future home.

Space

Orchids come in a broad range of sizes. If you want to keep several but have a tight space, opt for the miniature versions, as most thrive on windowsills. You can opt for standard-sized or slightly larger spaces if you have more space. The larger ones require a special stand, so keep this in mind when measuring how much space you have for them. Either way, see how much space you can allocate for your plants before buying them. You want to leave enough room for them to grow and bloom.

Adaptation

Some species are better at adapting to their environment, which is why they are often recommended for beginners. If you aren't sure how to choose the orchids based on your home's environment, you can never go wrong with the beginner-friendly species. If you're an experienced grower, you'll be better at picking plants based on your home environment, so you can choose whichever fits based on the above criteria.

How to Spot and Buy a Healthy Orchid at the Store

Whether you've discovered the perfect orchid match based on the above lists or hoping to find it when you arrive at the garden store, it's good to know how to spot a healthy plant. Knowing you bought one that fits you, but the plant still fails to thrive because it wasn't healthy when you purchased it can be incredibly frustrating. Avoid this by following the tips below.

Look at the Roots

Nothing will tell you more about a plant's health than its roots. Healthy orchid roots are firm and green. If the plant's roots are brown, it has likely been overwatered, which means it's not a healthy plant.

Notice the Leaves

Like the roots, the orchid's leaves should be bright green. If they're yellow, the plant isn't healthy. The orchid may have a few yellow leaves at the bottom and vibrant ones at the top. This is still a healthy plant. Plants lose mature leaves slowly, first by not putting as much chlorophyll in them (the cause of the yellow color), then by making them fall off. However, most leaves should not be pale green, yellow, or brown.

Also, if the plant has yellow spots on otherwise green leaves, this could be a sign of insect damage. If you notice these spots on the top of the leaves, look at their bottom, too. Bumps and web-like structures on the bottom of the leaves mean they were or are infested with insects.

Look at the Flowers

Always buy orchids with plenty of flowers and at least one new bud. The plant is thriving if the flowers look healthy and engorged and there are more in the growth phase (the buds). Make sure the flowers are attached to the spike. There is one more advantage if your orchid has buds besides the open flowers. You get to enjoy the blooming period for longer.

Glance at the Stems

Healthy orchids have strong spikes. Their flowers can be heavy (especially if there are many), so the stem must be able to sustain their weight. If the stem is bending because of the weight of the blooms, it's not strong enough, which means it's unhealthy.

Smell the Plant

After picking out a healthy-looking orchid plant, smell it. While many orchids don't have a scent, they shouldn't smell unpleasant. If they do, they aren't healthy. A rotting stem or root is usually responsible for the foul odor. If the plant looks healthy and doesn't have a smell (or has a pleasant scent), it will thrive with care.

Chapter 3: Potting and Repotting Orchids

In this chapter, you'll learn about the ins and outs of potting and repotting orchids. You'll find tips on choosing the right pot and medium and avoiding making mistakes that could severely stress out your beautiful orchid plants.

18. Pot your orchids the right way so they can grow properly. Source: https://www.pexels.com/photo/white-orchid-flowers-in-flowerpot-20723167/

Choosing the Right Pot: Plastic, Clay, or Hanging Baskets?

The first question many face is whether to use plastic or clay pots. While plastic pots are relatively inexpensive, they don't last long, especially if your plant is exposed to the sun most of the time. They retain more water, though, which could mean a vast difference with high moisture-dependent plants. Moreover, plastic pots can help avoid temperature loss in colder climates.

Transparent plastic pots are also good for small orchids if you aren't sure when to repot them. You can see if the roots began to creep toward the side or become tangled and overcrowded at the bottom. Also, if you must dismantle the pot to release a root-bound plant, it will be easier with a plastic one.

Clay pots, on the other hand, are more expensive and long-lasting. They keep roots cool in warmer climates and are sturdier due to their weight. They're recommended for larger plants in windy climates. Clay pots are also more breathable, which is great for orchids requiring heavy airflow.

Whether clay or plastic, the pots you use for your orchids must have drainage holes in the bottom. Sometimes, instead of (or in addition) to the small holes at the bottom, the pots will also have slits at the side of the bottom quarter. While many species enjoy high-moisture soil, lack of drainage can cause their roots to become waterlogged, which leads to root rot. Lack of drainage can also lead to the proliferation of disease-inducing microbes like bacteria or fungi.

If you can't decide between clear and opaque plastic pots, consider which orchid you are getting. For example, some adaptable species can use their roots for photosynthesis, further encouraging growth. For these, a transparent pot is a better choice. However, the plants won't be the only ones that grow faster in see-through containers — algae and weeds will, too (especially if the pot is outside).

When choosing the adequate pot size, it all comes down to whether you are potting or repotting. If you're repotting, choose a pot slightly bigger (usually an inch) than the previous one. This will allow the roots to expand and use all the medium.

If you're potting a new plant, you can choose from two pot dimensions recommended for orchids. One is wider than it is tall and is called the bulb pot. The other is the azalea pot, which is about the same height as its width. Extra large species will need an ultra-tall pot much taller than it is wide. When choosing the right pot size, allow for two years of growth unless it's a miniature orchid with moss as a medium. Those need smaller pots because they need to be repotted every year.

Another benefit of plastic pots is that you can put them into decorative containers. If you use decorative pots, note that these usually do not have drainage holes and slits. When watering, always remove the plastic pot from the decorative one, wait until the water drains, then return it to the decorative pot.

You can also choose from standing or hanging pots. The latter looks very appealing (even if they're plastic or clay) and may even help with faster drainage. The water will leave faster due to gravity, so calculate this into your water schedule. However, hanging pots can also save space, whereas standing pots provide more stability for larger plants.

Best Orchid Potting Mediums and Their Uses

Potting mediums are essential for growing plants. They provide nutrients, moisture, and airflow to the roots, allowing them to drain properly. You'll have a wide variety to choose from when it comes to potting mediums for orchids. While the most common medium these plants thrive on are bark, moss, and fern, the number of combinations incorporating these is large.

Bark

Made from redwood tree or Douglas fir bark, Orchid bark is perfect for infrequent repotting. It takes a long time to decay but drains rapidly, which your orchids will appreciate.

Moss

Moss, more specifically sphagnum moss, does the opposite. Instead of draining it, it binds water. This helps the orchids absorb enough water through the roots. Moss is also a fungal repellent, which can help prevent plant diseases. The only downside of moss is that it deteriorates fast and is only suitable for annual repotting.

Fern Roots

Also known as tree fern, fern roots are rough and slow to decay. They only need to be repotted every three years, and they drain quickly like bark. It's a little more expensive, but considering its infrequent replacement, it can be a good choice for larger orchids.

Bark, Charcoal, and Coarse Perlite Mix

This mixture is ideal for orchids with high moisture and humidity needs. It allows the roots to remain hydrated and grow, making it perfect for beginners. The charcoal in it helps contain diseases and purifies the soil. It also prevents the roots from becoming waterlogged. The perlite contributes to adequate airflow and water retention for the plants.

Bark Mixture with Chunky Peats

This mix is designed to retain nutrients and water, making it an excellent choice for high humidity-dependent orchids. It's often used for both indoor and outdoor growing, where tropical conditions can be naturally or artificially simulated.

Bark, Charcoal, Coarse Perlite, and Lava Rock Combo

Similar to the first mixture, except it breaks down even slower, thanks to the lava rock. This guarantees optimal aeration and water flow because the soil does not condense easily. It is best used for orchids that thrive in moisture-abundant soil and require frequent watering. It prevents their roots from drying out, which is a huge plus.

Which medium you pick also depends on the size of your orchid. For example, if your plant requires a three or four-inch pot, it will thrive on a simple 50:50 bark-fir mixture. If your plant is even smaller, choosing sphagnum moss is a good idea because you'll likely need to repot it within a year anyway (smaller plants use up resources more quickly). Whereas, if your orchids need a pot eight inches or larger, they'll do better in a coarse mixture. You likely won't repot them too often, and you'll have a medium with optimal drainage for the larger root system.

When and How to Repot Orchids

Most orchids need repotting every 2-3 years to refresh their rootage. However, it will depend on when it becomes root-bound. How do you notice this? Remove the orchid from its pot and look at the roots. If they are twisted and tangled together, it's time to repot.

You'll also need to repot when your potting medium has a foul smell. This is a sign of decay, and it occurs when the plant has used all the nutrients from the soil. Likewise, you may also need to transplant your orchid into a new pot when it has outgrown the old one. You'll know when this happens because the roots start appearing on the top or side of the soil. The bottom has become too crowded, and they're trying to find space higher up.

How to Repot Orchids

Supplies:

- A new pot
- Medium
- Water
- Pruning shears (optional)

Instructions:

1. When using a new pot, prepare it first. Fill it with a medium around ⅓ of the way.

2. Remove the orchid from its original pot. Be careful not to break off any rootage close to the plants. However, if your plant has become root-bound, you can cut off some of the root system around the periphery. It will likely die anyway. Alternatively, if the roots are very overgrown, you may need to cut open the original pot to remove the plant.

3. Place the orchid into the new pot, positioning it in the center. You can use a different pot, or, if you haven't cut

it and its size is still adequate, clean the old one and use that again. If your plant is root-bound, you'll need a larger pot, which means reaching for a different one.

4. Fill the spaces between the roots, then cover the entire rootage with the medium.
5. Water the soil generously.

Avoiding Repotting Shock: Step-by-Step Guide

Your orchids are used to taking in a specific amount of water. If they can't do that from their new pot, they'll suffer the effects of water stress (or shock). It can damage the plant's roots, so it's best to avoid it.

Here is how you can minimize the chances of repotting shock:

1. Start the reporting process in a high-temperature and humidity environment. Dry air and low temperatures make it harder for the plant to take in water.
2. Prepare the pot with your preferred medium before you start repotting. The longer the plant is out of a pot, the more its roots dry out.
3. Water your plant to ensure its roots remain hydrated during transplanting.
4. While removing the plant from its pot, take as many roots as possible. The more roots, the more opportunity to take in water.
5. Try not to disturb the orchid's roots too much when you remove it from the pot. Avoid giving into the temptation of shaking off the excess dirt.

6. Place the plant into the prepared pot. Then, surround its roots with more medium.

7. Press the soil around the plant so the roots can dig into the soil from all sides and start taking in water.

8. Water the new soil as soon as you've planted the orchids so the plants have enough water to absorb.

Chapter 4: Watering and Humidity – The Most Common Orchid Issue

One of the first questions plant owners ask is how often they should water their orchids. Some people think you should water them daily. Others believe watering plants once a week is enough. You should know how much water your orchid needs and recognize the signs that your plant is overwatered or underwatered, or you will risk damaging it.

19. Learning about humidity and how to water your orchids is imperative to their health. Source: https://unsplash.com/photos/water-pouring-on-gray-steel-watering-can-P7saq8j11pM

Humidity is another factor that can kill or help your plant thrive. You should know the safe levels for orchids and create an accommodating environment for them.

This chapter explains how often you should water orchids, signs of overwatering and underwatering, solutions to fix these issues, best watering techniques, and tips to create the perfect humid environment.

How Often Should You Water Different Orchid Types?

Each orchid species has different watering needs. Orchids with thin leaves and roots should be watered more frequently than orchids with big leaves, thick roots, and pseudobulbs. Pseudobulb orchids such as Dendrobium orchid, Cattleya orchid, and Oncidium orchid can retain moisture more than others, so they don't need to be watered frequently.

The Phalaenopsis orchid is one of the most popular species. It has big leaves and thick roots but doesn't retain water, so you should test the soil regularly to ensure it doesn't dry out.

Orchids without pseudobulbs, such as Paphiopedilum orchid and Vanda orchid, should be watered more frequently. Some species should always be moist, such as the Cymbidium and monkey orchids, so they will require more watering.

Check the label on your plant if you aren't sure about its watering frequency, and follow the instructions to avoid damaging your orchid. However, most species should be watered once a week in winter and twice in the summer. The pot's size also impacts your plant's watering needs. For instance, if your plant is in a four-inch pot, water it every five to six days. If it is in a six-inch pot, you can water it every week.

The potting medium also affects watering frequency. If you use a dense soil-based mix, water your orchid less frequently than when using a well-draining mix, sphagnum moss, or potting bark.

Humidity and temperature also play a role. You should water your orchid less frequently if you live in low-humidity areas with low temperatures. This is unlike warm areas with high humidity that require more frequent watering.

Keeping a watering schedule can be hard if you live in an area where the humidity and weather are constantly changing. In this case, you must check on your plant regularly to see if it needs more water.

Make sure to water the orchid's mix thoroughly, leaving it moist. Don't rehydrate the plant until it dries out. Put your finger in the bark or moss to check if it is dry. You can also use a chopstick or a pencil.

Watering Orchids Grown in Moss

Water orchids that grow in sphagnum moss from the top, just like other house plants. Sphagnum moss retains moisture, so it will be damp inside the pot but dry on the surface, making you think your plant is thirsty. You should test it using a pencil or finger to see if the soil is dry or moist.

The moss should remain moist but not too moist, or the plant will rot.

Instructions:

1. Put the orchid's pot under the faucet until it flows through the draining holes.

2. Don't soak the part of the orchid where the leaves attach to the stem.
3. Water it every week or when the moss dries out.

Watering Orchids Grown in Wood or Bark Chips

Sprinkling bark orchids may not work because you need to soak the bark pieces. Wood and bark chips don't retain water, so they should be soaked in water.

Instructions:

1. Cover the plant with water just below the top.
2. Make sure the whole pot is soaked evenly.
3. Let it drain out.
4. Water the plant every four to ten days or when the bark dries.

Watering Orchids Grown in Tree Fern Fiber

Tree fern is one of the main components of orchid potting mixes. It retains water more than bark chips.

Instructions:

1. Soak it under faucet water like the sphagnum moss and let it drain out.
2. When the pot becomes lighter and the fiber color becomes lighter, it indicates that the fiber dries out and needs watering.

Watering Orchids Grown in Clay Pellets, Charcoal, Rocks, and Gravel

Clay pellets, charcoal, rocks, and gravel don't retain water and require watering more often.

Instructions:

1. Put the orchid pot under the faucet until the water flows from the holes.
2. Leave the plant for 15 minutes to dry.
3. Water the plant once a week to protect the roots from drying out.

Overwatering vs. Underwatering – Signs and Fixes

You should recognize the signs of overwatering and underwatering because they can cause serious problems and damage your plants.

Signs of Overwatered Plants

- Brown or black spots on leaves
- Mold or algae in the potting mix
- Bad smell coming from the potting mix
- Mushy, soft roots
- Yellowing or wilting leaves
- Thin leaves
- Mushy, brown roots
- Yellow stems

Solutions for Overwatered Plant

Instructions:

1. Gently remove the plant from the pot.

2. If the roots are mushy and black or brown, trim them with pruning shears or sharp scissors. Leave the healthy roots.
3. Clean your work surface, scissors or pruners, and hands to prevent infection. You can also use gloves to prevent contamination.
4. Remove the infected leaves and dead pieces of the stem.
5. Treat the plant with fungicide to prevent further infections.
6. Apply it on the roots and soil and follow the instructions on the label.
7. Repot the plant in a new and clean growing medium. If you don't have a new one, you can use the old one, but you must rub it with alcohol or clean it with warm water to disinfect it.
8. Don't water your plant again until it dries out.
9. If the stem turns yellow, it may be hard to save the plant.

If you don't overwater it, you may be able to save the roots instead of trimming them.

Instructions:

1. Take the plant out and check the roots to see if they are rotting. If they are, refer to the previous steps; if not, proceed.
2. Let the roots dry out.
3. Put the plant back in the pot.

4. Adjust the watering schedule and reduce the watering frequency.
5. If there was minimal root rot, water the orchids every week or ten days.

Signs of Under-Watered Plants
- Lack of growth of new flowers and leaves
- Shriveled pseudobulbs
- Flower buds falling off instead of opening
- Slow or stunted growth
- Gray roots
- Wrinkled leaves
- Dry, crispy leaves

Solutions for Underwatered Plant
- Use the ice-cube method to guarantee that your plant always gets enough water.
- Check the roots to make sure that your orchid is getting enough water. Healthy roots are flexible and bright green.
- Dry roots are gray or white and brittle. Dehydrate immediately if so.
- Create a new and improved watering schedule that guarantees your orchid gets enough water. You can check the instructions on the plant or test the soil every day or two and water to see if it is dry.
- Roots may dry out if the plant is near a drafty area or a vent. Put it in a place with consistent temperature.

- Water the roots then check it in a day or two. If it is silver or white, your orchid is dry and absorbs water fast.
- If you tried the previous steps and the roots are still dry, soak them with the bark in the sink for two minutes.
- Drain before returning it to the pot.

Best Watering Techniques

Now that you understand the importance of watering plants, you can learn different techniques and find which works best.

Misting

Orchids are tropical plants so they thrive in the humidity. Mist the plants with a spray bottle to create a similar environment. Spray the leaves twice a day to make sure it is hydrated. To be safe, check the soil with a pencil before misting. Don't mist if it is damp or wet. Use distilled water instead of tap water.

Signs Your Orchid Needs a Mist

- Twister flowers
- Brown spots on leaves
- Flower buds falling off
- Slow growth

Soaking

Soaking is the best technique when your orchids are dehydrated.

Instructions:

1. Fill a large bowl with water and soak the orchid's pot in it.
2. Let the water level reach just below the pot's lip to prevent the bark's mix from spilling out.
3. Soak for ten minutes.
4. Let the water drain out. While orchids can tolerate soaking, they can wither in sitting water.

Ice Cubes

This may seem unorthodox, but it is effective and has become very popular. Although orchids don't fare well in the freezing weather, this technique is safe and prevents overwatering and underwatering.

This method is perfect for people who don't know how to keep their plants hydrated, are busy and can't stick to a watering schedule, or struggle with keeping orchids alive.

Instructions:

1. Put one ice cube on top of the bark in the winter and two or three ice cubes in the summer. Make sure they don't touch the leaves or stems.
2. Drain the excess water after the ice cubes melt.
3. Check the roots. If they are bright green, your plant is hydrated.

So, which one should you choose? Each method has its uses. Use the misting technique if you live in an area with low humidity. Soaking is the right method for people who constantly underwater, while the ice cube method is for people who over-water or under-water their plants. They are all effective so choose the right one for you.

How to Create the Perfect Humidity for Orchids

Placing your orchid in the wrong place can affect it's growth. The important thing to remember is that orchid's need humidity to thrive, so follow these tips to help you create the right environment for your flowers.

Control the Temperature

Most orchid species don't fare well in temperatures below 60 °F, so keep your home between 60 °F and 80 °F.

Increase the Humidity

Increase the humidity if you live in dry areas. Fill a tray with gravel and pour water until it is half full to keep the pot on the gravel instead of in the water. Check it every few hours and add water to the tray when necessary.

You can also use a humidifier for the orchids. Follow the instructions on the humidifier's label to prevent moisture accumulation. Clean it regularly to protect your home against bacterial and fungal growth.

You can also mist the leaves twice a day.

Increase Airflow at Home

Place a fan near your orchid to improve the air movement at your home. Open windows and doors to let in the fresh air and keep your home properly ventilated. Airflow protects against fungi, bacteria, mold, and diseases.

Track Humidity Levels

Use a humidistat to track the humidity levels in your home. It helps you adjust the humidity levels so they don't get too high or too low.

Meet the Orchid Humidity Requirements

Most homes' humidity levels are between 30 and 50%, while the ideal humidity for orchids such as Laelia, Phalaenopsis, Paphiopedilum, Cattleya, and Oncidium is between 50 and 80. If you want to grow any of these orchids, you must adjust your home's humidity levels.

However, if the humidity in your home is between 35 and 40%, you can grow Laelia – purpurata group, Catasetum, and Dendrobium kingianum.

Watering your orchid properly is key to a healthy and blooming plant. Avoid overwatering or underwatering your flower or you will risk killing it. Use the watering technique you prefer, but stick to a schedule. Create a humid environment for your orchid to grow and bloom.

Keep your eyes on the plant soil and only water it when it is dry unless it's an orchid species that should always be moist.

Chapter 5: Light and Temperature – Creating the Ideal Growing Environment

This chapter focuses on light and temperature settings, the ultimate tools for managing orchid health. It shows you how to create the optimal orchid-growing environment by finding the right lighting setup and understanding how light and temperature affect these precious plants.

20. Light and temperature need to be just right for your orchids to grow. Source: https://commons.wikimedia.org/wiki/File:Phototropism.jpg

Understanding Light Requirements for Different Orchid Types

Most orchids are resilient and can adapt to various growing conditions. However, after water and humidity, the most important factors to consider when nurturing these plants are light and temperature. For the same reason, you can only grow healthy orchid plants if you put them in a place where the light conditions are favorable.

Most orchids need at least a moderate amount of light. Indoors, they can get this when placed near windows. Alternatively, this can be provided through artificial lighting. Some orchids require low-light conditions, like most bathrooms. Others prefer higher light exposure, meaning they should be exposed to light daily. An easy solution is to find a south-facing position for them, as this could give them six or more hours of sunlight a day.

Without enough light, your orchids won't bloom. The more light they require, the more they'll struggle to grow flowers without adequate exposure. With so many species and varieties available, how do you decide whether your plant receives enough light or needs more or less?

If you aren't sure how much light to provide, look at how your orchids respond to their current light exposure. What is the color of their leaves? Is it light or vivid green? If yes, they receive just enough light. If it's dark green, the plants need more light. If the leaves are pale, the orchids have too much light exposure.

Best Indoor Lighting Setups (Natural and Artificial Light Solutions)

Light intensity is crucial for making orchids bloom. The higher the light intensity, the more energy a plant will have. If exposed to low-intensity light, the plant will have weak stems that will buckle under their own weight. Conversely, exposure to too high light intensity can cause burn damage on the orchid's leaves. This reduces the surface areas the plant has for photosynthesis and energy production. To avoid this, the intensity of the light must be just right. Once the plants have enough energy, they'll convert it into flowers.

Besides light intensity, duration of exposure and light quality can also determine whether your orchids will thrive. The spectrum of wavelengths determines light quality (you see these as lights in different colors) projected at an object.

Outside or in a greenhouse, orchids usually get enough good-quality light. However, this may not be the case if grown indoors — whether under artificial lights or natural lighting through windows. For example, did you know that some windows are designed to prevent UV light from penetrating them? Or that some artificial light sources only emit certain wavelengths?

Natural Light Solutions

Location is the primary factor in getting the best natural light solution for growing orchids indoors. You want to place the orchid where it gets just the right quality and intensity of lighting and for just as long as it needs it. This can depend from one species to another. For example, while some will thrive on windowsills, placing others near the windows can be contraindicative. You should also consider the position of the window. Depending on the direction your window faces, you can achieve great variations in light exposure durations and intensity.

In the northern hemisphere, south-facing windows provide the highest intensity and quality of lighting. You can give them over 5 hours of light exposure by placing your orchids in south-facing windows. West-facing ones provide moderate quality, while east-facing ones supply lower-quality light. Placed in west and east-facing windows, your plants will be exposed to light 2-5 hours a day. The lowest quality and intensity you get is from north-facing windows. Placed here, your plants get less than 2 hours of light exposure.

You'll want to place the plant 2-3 feet away from the window, especially if you have south or west-facing windows. You don't want them to be in the middle of the room either because they won't have enough light. The key is to find a happy medium that works for the plant.

You also want to place the orchids in line with the window to ensure they get the full spectrum of the light exposure the window provides. If you put them next to or not in line with the window, they won't get the same quality and intensity of lighting that enters the space directly through the window.

Besides looking at their leaves, you can measure the intensity of the light your orchid is getting through the window via an app or the hand-in-front-of-paper method. Hold a piece of paper where you want to measure light intensity and place your other hand 8-10 inches away from it. If you can see a clear or soft-edged outline of your hand, the light is too intense and probably harmful to your plants. If you see a blurred outline of your hand, the light is moderate and most likely suitable for orchid species that prefer medium to high light exposure. If you can barely see the outline of your hand, the light is very low intensity and only suitable for species thriving in low light conditions.

Artificial Light Solutions

Artificial lights are more customizable than natural light sources, allowing you to grow more species and varieties. You may be able to cultivate orchids you couldn't before because you didn't have adequate natural light conditions for them. You may also see more flowers on your orchids. Some orchids are very delicate and require specialized care to flower. With a growth light system, you can start seeing species that only bloomed once previously flower several times a year.

Also, if you grow your orchids on the windowsill, they can get too much light exposure during the summer. To avoid this, you can close the blinds and expose your plants to artificial light until the lighting isn't as intense.

Artificial light solutions have become inexpensive, making growing orchids in any indoor environment very convenient. You can choose between fluorescent, LED, incandescent, and high-pressure sodium lights when looking for artificial lighting solutions.

Incandescent lights don't provide enough light quality or intensity to sustain healthy orchid growth and flowering. On the other hand, high-pressure sodium lights are so powerful that they can only be used in greenhouses. They generate extremely high temperatures but provide a full spectrum of light.

Due to their wide spectrum of colors and ability to diffuse the light, fluorescent lights are popular among orchid growers. If you want to use them, remember they can get very hot, so make sure no leaves or other plant parts touch them. Also, they shouldn't be closer than about 2 feet to plants. You can achieve the best results with bulbs that have a color range (temperature) of 5000-6500 K, Color Rendering Index (CRI) of 85-90, and high lumen output (shine the brightest).

LED lights have also become widespread for indoor plant-growing uses. Their benefit is they don't get as hot. However, they can't diffuse the light and can still burn plants if kept too close. You also have to buy special plant-growing LED bulbs because the others can be extremely low quality and won't help nurture your orchids. When picking up your plant-growing LEDs, ensure they are full spectrum, i.e., distribute blue, green, red, and far-red light.

Tips for Using Artificial Lights

The number one tip is to put your lights on a timer. This way, you can provide your orchids the amount of exposure they require without having to remember to turn your light on and off. After letting them rest overnight, your timer can start in the morning and work for 12-14 hours.

Depending on where you set up your lights, some orchids may get more exposure than others. For example, tall varieties will get more exposure to a light source above them. Similarly, smaller orchids will do better when exposed from the side.

If you're using fluorescent lights, the plants directly under the light source will be exposed to the highest light intensity. If you have species that require lower light intensity, place them slightly off from the center of the light source.

If you want to maximize your plant's light exposure, you can rotate them occasionally toward the light source. Since they grow toward the light, you will make them grow straighter and faster if you keep rotating them and exposing all their sides to the light. This technique can be applied to both artificial and natural light sources indoors.

Alternatively, you can place mirrors across the room from the light source. Be careful to put them at an angle where they don't project the light directly onto the plants, as this can burn them. Instead, position the mirrors to illuminate the places previously in the shadow.

How Seasonal Temperature Changes Affect Orchids

Even though most care tips for different orchids apply all year round, seasonal changes can cause owners to tweak their care routine. Besides the temperature changes across the seasons, humidity levels can also fluctuate at different times. This can affect the health of your orchids even if they grow inside.

What specific changes should you account for? Outside temperatures can drop significantly in winter, and while heating becomes essential for you and your orchid, it can also dry out the air. Moreover, the number of daylight hours shortens, bringing out the need for artificial lighting. Otherwise, your orchids won't generate enough energy to grow those beautiful blossoms due to the colder temperatures and lack of light exposure.

When spring comes, your orchids can take advantage of gradually lengthening days, warmer temperatures, and increased humidity. All this will kick start their growth very quickly. However, weather conditions can fluctuate very rapidly during the spring. Sudden temperature drops can still occur, which can cause stress to your plants. Another source of springtime stress for them is the appearance of insects. Many insects wake up with nature after hibernation, ready to find plants and other sources of food to continue or begin their life cycle. For all these reasons, monitoring your orchids' health closely during the spring is a good idea. The goal is to prevent them from suffering shock from inconsistent weather and insect activity.

During the summer, weather conditions are more stable, but your orchids may encounter other difficulties. While they have tropical origins, overexposure to extreme heat can damage them, especially when combined with low humidity. Your plants will need additional care, including increased watering, protection against direct sunlight exposure, and monitoring for burns. Insects are also active during the summer and can cause as much damage as they do during the spring.

In the fall, temperatures drop again, and your orchids can enjoy moderately warm temperatures at the beginning of the season. However, as you go deeper into fall, temperatures start dropping even more, and so will the length of sunlight hours. Monitoring whether your orchids are getting enough sunlight is a good idea. It can help you continue keeping them in bloom.

Orchids have different ways of adapting to seasonal changes. Moreover, not all of them are affected by the temperature and humidity fluctuations in the same way. For example, some prefer very high daytime temperatures and very cold nights. To them, getting through the summer months when night temperatures are significantly higher will be challenging. Without the cooler night temperatures, they likely won't flower. Whereas during the winter, they'll thrive under long exposure to artificial lighting and dark, cool nights when the lights are turned off.

Other orchids, native to territories with fewer temperature fluctuations, won't be affected as much by seasonal variations. Before buying your orchids, research where the species or variety originates from so you can prepare for whatever seasonal variations they may be affected by.

Chapter 6: Fertilizing and Feeding Orchids

Every plant has different fertilizing and nutrient needs. Understanding these needs is crucial to having fully grown and blooming flowers. New plant owners may not recognize malnutrition in their orchids. You may think that water provides your plant with enough nourishment and that it may not need anything else. However, like any other living organism, plants require feeding to survive.

21. Orchids need the right kind of nutrition from feeding and fertilizers. Source:

https://commons.wikimedia.org/wiki/File:Liparis_latifolia_OrchidsBln0906c.jpg

This chapter explains the orchid's nutrient needs, the best fertilizer options, how and when to fertilize your flowers, and tips for recognizing nutrient deficiencies and solving them.

Understanding Orchid Nutrient Needs

House orchids get their nutrients from the water and the environment you create for them, such as lighting, humidity, and temperature. However, this isn't always enough. Orchids need fertilizers for maximum blooming, optimal health, and strong immunity. Plants that don't get enough nutrients are weak, prone to diseases and pests, and don't grow or bloom.

Orchids require macronutrients such as sulfur, magnesium, calcium, potassium, phosphorus, nitrogen, oxygen, hydrogen, and carbon in large amounts. They also need smaller amounts of micronutrients such as chloride, nickel, zinc, molybdenum, manganese, iron, copper, and boron. Each of these elements plays a role in helping the plant produce sugar, form chlorophyll, break down carbohydrates, boost metabolism, and improve reproduction.

Plants get a daily supply of oxygen, hydrogen, and carbon from water and air but don't have access to other elements. Fertilizers contain many mineral elements that can give your orchids the necessary nutrients.

Fertilizer packages often have the letters "NPK," which stands for nitrogen, phosphorus, and potassium because they are the most significant minerals. You will also find their percentage on the label. Nitrogen aids in leaf growth, phosphorus increases budding and flowering, and potassium strengthens the roots.

Magnesium and calcium boosts flower formation and cellular functions. However, you may not find these two macronutrients in NPK fertilizers, so read the label before purchasing. Fertilizers that only contain nitrogen, phosphorus, and potassium are of low quality. You must ensure that the fertilizer you choose contains both macronutrients and micronutrients.

Best Orchid Fertilizers

There are different types of fertilizers, and you are probably wondering which is the best for your plant. This part focuses on the liquid, granular, and organic options to help you choose the right one for your orchid.

Liquid Fertilizer

Liquid fertilizers have many advantages. They are easily dissolved and absorbed, strengthen the plants, and boost their growth. They also contain the essential elements: nitrogen, phosphorus, potassium, and other important nutrients.

Types of Liquid Fertilizers

- **NPK Fertilizers:** The most popular liquid fertilizers because they contain the three most important nutrients.

- **Micronutrient Fertilizers:** Although they are required in smaller amounts, these are necessary for plants' overall health.

- **Organic Liquid Fertilizers:** They are made from manure, fish emulsion, and other organic ingredients. This type is ideal for plant owners who prefer natural over chemical options.

- **Foliar Fertilizers:** You spray these fertilizers directly on the orchids' leaves to be absorbed through the foliage. They enhance the plants' growth and give them the nutrients they need. They also fix nutrient deficiencies and protect against pests and diseases.

How to Apply Liquid Fertilizers

- **Pressure Sprayer:** This method applies the fertilizers directly on the plant making it ideal for foliar fertilizers.
- **Water Can:** It is perfect for potted plants allowing for direct application to the orchids' base.

Benefits of Liquid Fertilizers

- **Low Risk of Burns:** Liquid fertilizers are diluted with water to protect the plants from burning, which can occur due to high nutrient concentrations.
- **Fast and Easy:** They are easy to apply, and plants absorb them quickly.
- **Compatibility and Frequency of Application:** You can mix different types of liquid fertilizers and apply them to the plant. This provides your orchids with a large variety of nutrients.

Granular Fertilizers

Granular fertilizers are uniform and small granules that can be easily applied, handled, and stored. They contain nitrogen, phosphorus, and potassium mixed with micronutrients and formed into dissolvable granules. You put them in the soil and they will dissolve slowly, providing your plant with essential nutrients to enhance their health and growth.

Types of Granular Fertilizers

- **Nitrogen-Based:** These fertilizers contain high levels of nitrogen, which aid in leaf development and vegetative growth. They are easily dissolved in water, allowing the plants to absorb the nutrients right away.

- **Phosphorus-Based:** They help with flowering, developing roots, early growth, root development, and transferring energy to the rest of the plant. They also improve quality and flower production.

- **Potassium-Based:** These fertilizers can protect the plants against pests, heat, drought, and disease. They help form proteins, starches, and sugar.

- **Specialty Granular Fertilizers:** They tailor nutrients to plants' specific needs with a mix of macronutrients and micronutrients. They help improve imbalances and deficiencies to improve soil's health.

Benefits of Granular Fertilizers:

- **Versatility:** Granular fertilizers come in various forms tailored to many plant nutrient requirements. They also contain the three main nutrients with micronutrients that cater to different soil types.

- **Improves Soil Health:** These fertilizers raise nutrient levels in the soil and promote microbial activity. They also improve nutrient cycles and soil fertility.

- **Easy Application and Handling:** Their small size makes them easy to handle, apply, and store. You can also distribute them using multiple methods, such as specialized equipment, banding, and broadcasting.

This allows for uniform, efficient, and even distribution.

- **Nutrient Targeting:** Granular fertilizers can target plants' specific nutrient needs. This guarantees that all types of plants get the required elements in the right quantities for strong health and optimal growth.

Organic Fertilizers

Organic fertilizers are compost made from plant and animal residue or waste. They are natural and don't contain any chemicals.

Types of Organic Fertilizers

- **Animal-Based Fertilizers:** These are made from animal bones and contain high levels of calcium and phosphorus. They help seedlings and flowers grow and increase yield. Blood fertilizers are made from dried animals' blood and can increase nitrogen levels in the soil. Animal manure can protect against fungi and improve soil's moisture retention abilities. Fish fertilizers increase nitrogen levels, and shellfish fertilizers are rich in phosphorus and calcium and can boost root growth and flower blooming.

- **Plant-Based Fertilizers:** Seaweed fertilizers contain iron and zinc. Soybean and alfalfa are rich in phosphorus and nitrogen. Cottonseed fertilizers contain nitrogen, phosphorus, and potassium. Compost improves soil fertility and helps retain water, promoting plant growth.

- **Mineral Fertilizers:** Rock Phosphate contains micronutrients and phosphate. Greensand is rich in magnesium, potassium, and iron. It helps soil retain water and flowers bloom.

Benefits of Organic Fertilizers

- Environmentally friendly
- Enhances aeration, drainage, and soil texture
- Increases organic matter and nutrient efficiency

How and When to Fertilize for Maximum Blooms

Fertilize orchids before flower buds appear, which is during vegetative growth. Stop fertilizing after the orchid begins to bloom and finishes its next dormant cycle to begin a new growth cycle. After the vegetative growth, you can fertilize for three weeks, stop for one, and so on.

How to Fertilize Orchids

- Don't mix orchid flower fertilizers with tap water. Use distilled water or rain water instead.
- Don't overfeed the orchids because this can do more harm than good. Non-organic fertilizers contain mineral salts that can build up in the pot. Overfed orchids bloom less and grow quickly but become weak and prone to diseases.
- Cattleya and some other orchid species' growth slows during the winter, while species such as Dendrobium become inactive. There is no need to fertilize inactive plants. Wait until they start growing again in the spring to fertilize.

Recognizing Nutrient Deficiencies and Fixing Them

Signs of Nutrient Deficiency in Plants

- Yield difference
- Stunted roots
- Twisted leaves
- Yellow or brown spots on leaves
- Small or stunted leaves
- Yellowing on leaves
- Red or purple spots on leaves
- Holes in leaves
- Leaves look burnt
- Yellow or brown leaves

Solutions

- Before treating your plant for nutrient deficiency, rule out other factors that could affect its health. Check for worms, spider mites, or grey mold.
- Check the soil to see if it is dry or wet, and determine if you have been overwatering or underwatering the plant.
- Check the humidity and temperature to ensure they are suitable for growing orchids.
- If your plant suffers from nitrogen deficiency, the lower leaves will turn yellow, shoots and branches will weaken, and purple stripes will appear on the stem.

Use a nitrogen-specific nutrient additive or organic fertilizers to treat it.

- In case of phosphorus deficiency, leaves will turn dark green with purple or red spots, growth will be affected, and leaves may turn brown. Use superphosphate, Phosphate Rock, or bone fertilizers to treat them.

- For potassium deficiency, leaves will turn brown and purple spots will also show on them. Fix it with organic fertilizers or additives like potassium sulfate.

- For calcium deficiency, leaves will wither and flowers will drop. Treat them with bone fertilizers.

- With magnesium deficiency, leaves will become pale, and their growth will be stunted. Treat plants with foliar spray fertilizer.

- With a sulfur deficiency, leaves will turn yellow, and the stem will turn purple. Use magnesium sulfate in foliar spray to treat them.

Fertilizers are plant food. They will sustain your orchid and keep it alive. Use -quality ones, read the ingredients to ensure they include all essential elements and constantly check for signs of deficiency.

Chapter 7: Common Orchid Problems and How to Fix Them

Do you struggle with keeping your orchid alive? Is it not blooming? You may be doing everything right and still having problems. Understandably, this can be frustrating and discourage you from growing plants. Luckily, there is a solution for every problem.

This chapter explains common orchid problems, such as yellowing leaves, buds falling off before blooming, dehydration, root rot, and diseases. You will also find solutions for each issue and tips about pest control.

Yellowing Leaves – Causes and Solutions

Orchid leaves turn yellow for different reasons. Understanding the causes of this discoloration will help you address the issue accordingly and protect the plant from further damage.

22. *Orchid leaves yellow for a variety of reasons. Source: https://commons.wikimedia.org/wiki/File:Bacterial_leaf_blight_o rchid_caused_by_Erwinia_sp._(5832793177).jpg*

Bacterial and Fungal Infections

Bacterial and fungal infections can change the leaf color and cause root rot, black rot, and spotting.

Solutions

Trim the infected leaves and other parts that look unhealthy to prevent the spread of bacteria and fungus. Adjust humidity and create a well-ventilated environment for your orchid that allows good airflow. Leave an adequate space between your plants to prevent infections. Use bactericides or fungicides if the infections are severe.

Pests

Spider mites, mealybugs, insects, aphids, and other pests can cause serious issues to the leaves. Pests feed on nutrients in the orchids' sap, causing yellow spots on small areas. Those can quickly spread and change the leaves' color. This will weaken the flower and cause various health problems.

You should treat pest issues immediately or they will damage the whole plant, not only the leaves. The stem will weaken, discoloration will spread, and the flowers won't bloom.

Solutions

Water the plant with a spray bottle or spray nozzle. You need strong water pressure to remove the pests from the leaves. However, it shouldn't be too strong or it will damage the plant. Use neem oil or insecticidal soap to control infestations. If the infestations are severe, you will need to use a stronger treatment like pesticides. Check the label to ensure it is suitable for orchids and follow the instructions.

Pests may come back, so constantly check on the leaves to see if there are any signs of infection.

Temperature

Low temperatures can cause serious stress to orchids, leading to yellowing leaves. High temperatures can cause equal damage. Placing the plant near direct sunlight can burn the leaves and change their color.

Solutions

Orchids thrive in stable temperatures between 65°F-75°F during the day and a slightly lower temperature at night. During the summer, keep the plant away from direct sunlight and drafty windows in the winter.

Poor Airflow

High humidity and poor air circulation can cause plant diseases and discoloration.

Solution

Improve airflow in your home by opening windows or putting a small fan near the orchid.

Nutritional Deficiencies

Healthy plants with green leaves get enough nutrients. However, yellow leaves can indicate that your plant isn't getting essential elements, specifically nitrogen. Magnesium and calcium deficiencies can also cause leaf discoloration, mainly in young leaves. Iron deficiency can lead to discoloration between the veins.

Solution

Ensure your orchid gets enough nutrients by giving it a balanced, water-soluble fertilizer.

Light Stress

Plants weaken if they don't get enough light and turn yellow if exposed to intense direct sunlight.

Solution

Find a place for your orchid to get bright but indirect sunlight. If you have to put it near a window, place a sheer curtain to protect it.

Underwatering

Dehydration is one of the most common reasons behind yellowing leaves.

Solution

Water your plant more frequently. The potting medium should always be moist, not dry or soggy. You can also soak the plant if it is too dry.

Overwatering

Overwatering orchids can cause many issues, including yellowing leaves.

Solutions

Trim the brown and infected roots and place the orchid in a fresh and clean pot. Check the soil before watering and make sure it is partially dry.

Aging

Just like people, plants get old. Yellow leaves can indicate aging and at the end of their life cycle.

Solution

Remove the dead leaves to keep the plant looking healthy.

Buds Falling Off Before Blooming – What's Wrong?

Watching your flower buds fall before blooming can be frustrating. You took care of your plant, watered it, fertilized it, etc., but it was all in vain. However, buds don't fall off for no reason. Getting to the root of the problem will save the buds and give you beautiful and blooming flowers.

Genetics

You may give your plant the perfect environment, but buds still fall off before blooming. This can result from a genetic mutation that prevents the orchid from producing flowers.

Solutions

Nothing can be done here. You can't fix genetic mutation, so you must discard the plant.

Chemical Damage

Applying high doses of pesticides or fungicides can damage the buds.

Solutions

You can't stop using chemicals, especially when your plant gets infected with pests or fungi. However, you should check the instructions before applying them correctly. You can also try natural, safe options for you and your plant.

Atmosphere

Orchids are sensitive plants, and many chemicals in the atmosphere, like natural gas leaks and paint fumes, can impact them and cause serious damage. When flowers get pollinated, they release methane gas, causing them to collapse to save energy to produce seeds. Orchids may also be exposed to methane or ethylene gas from various sources such as smog, open fires, cigarette smoke, engine exhaust, perfume, gas leaks, and ripening fruit. All of which can lead to buds falling off.

Solutions

If you keep your orchids indoors, you can have more control over the environment. Make sure the air around your plant is fresh and clean. Keep your home properly ventilated, don't smoke near the orchid, or place the pot in the kitchen or near stoves or heaters. Don't place it near windows if you live in a polluted area.

Environmental Changes

A sudden change in the orchid's environment can be traumatic to the buds. For instance, it may take your orchid time to adjust to its new home, especially if it is accustomed to a different environment, such as a paradisiacal greenhouse. Expect to lose a few buds when you first bring it home.

Solution

You can't do much here. Be patient with your plant. It will eventually adjust. However, be careful about changing your orchid's environment regularly. For instance, moving your orchid to a different room can also affect the buds. Don't move the plant before the buds open.

Improper Fertilizing

Fertilizing plants is vital for keeping them alive and helping flowers bloom. However, too much fertilizer can cause burns and damage the orchid's buds.

Solution

Fertilize the orchid every week or two and stop fertilizing when it is dormant. Use liquid fertilizers suitable for orchids and follow the instructions on the label.

Root Rot vs. Dehydration – How to Diagnose and Fix

Root rot early symptoms can be hard to notice since they appear under the soil. You won't be able to see them until the issue spreads. Unhealthy roots are dry, mushy, and brown or black. Healthy roots are green, firm, and swollen with dark tips.

Many factors can contribute to root rot, such as fungal infections, poor airflow, bad drainage, overwatering, and maintenance issues.

Healthy roots absorb water and fertilizers from the soil to keep the plant alive. Damaged ones prevent the plant from getting nutrients, leading to poor health and death. You can treat the roots and save the orchid if root rot is caught early.

How to Diagnose Root Rot

- Pale or limp aerial roots, leaves, or stems.
- Flat, mushy, soft, or discolored roots
- Flower buds falling off before blooming
- Yellow leaves
- Dark spots on foliage
- Stunted growth

How to Fix Root Rot

Tools and Materials

- Sharp cutting tool
- Isopropyl alcohol
- Orcid fungicide
- Spray bottles
- Loose potting materials
- Orchid pot with drainage holes

Instructions:

1. Wear gloves and remove the orchid from the pot to examine the roots. If they are rotten, proceed to the next step.
2. Soak the roots in a small container, but don't get the foliage wet.
3. Drain off excess water and let the plant sit for 24 hours.

4. If you haven't removed the plant from the pot, water it thoroughly by running water through the pot for one minute.

5. To avoid fungal infections, ensure the roots are completely dry before working with them.

6. If the orchids are in the pot, gently remove them. Be careful not to damage the plant.

7. Use a butter knife or a chopstick and insert it in the pot. Run it around the edge of the pot to loosen the soil.

8. Tip the pot over and gently hold the plant by the stem's base.

9. If the orchid is in a plastic pot, squeeze both sides to loosen the dirt while pulling the plant out.

10. Place the orchid on a clean surface. You can sterilize wash and dry the surface beforehand.

11. Separate and remove rotten materials in the roots with your fingers.

12. Separate the unhealthy roots from the main stems.

13. Cut the base of the damaged roots with the cutting tool.

14. Sanitize your cutting tool with alcohol after each cut to avoid spreading the infection to the rest of the plant.

15. Keep cutting the damaged or partially damaged roots until healthy tissue appears.

16. Yellow roots are healthy; don't cut them.

17. Throw the soil and the damaged roots in the garbage.

18. Place the orchid in a new, clean, sterilized pot with new soil.

19. Leave the orchid for a week to recover. Don't water or fertilize.

Dehydration

How to Diagnose Dehydration

- Dry roots
- Wilted/wrinkled leaves
- Plant drooping

How to Fix Dehydration

Instructions:

1. Examine the orchid for signs of dehydration to assess the extent of the damage.
2. Soak the pot in room temperature water for 10 to 15 minutes. This allows the plant medium and roots to absorb the water and hydrate the orchid.
3. Remove from the water and let it drain out.
4. Choose a mix that won't dehydrate the orchid, such as perlite or sphagnum moss. This prevents the water from accumulating around the roots and causing dehydration.
5. Trim the roots and repot the orchid.
6. Place the orchid away from direct sunlight and increase humidity to prevent dehydration.
7. Don't fertilize until the plants recover and start growing again.

Pest Control for Orchids – Natural and Chemical Solutions

All plants are prone to pest infections. You can choose between natural and chemical pesticides to treat your orchid. If left untreated, insects and fungus can spread and damage the plant.

Natural Solutions

Natural treatments are healthier because they don't contain harmful chemicals.

- **Eucalyptus Oil:** It is an environmentally safe and natural insecticide and pesticide. It protects plants against insects, mites, and fungi.
- **Pyrethrum:** It comes from the Chrysanthemum flowers and is one of the strongest natural pesticides. Pyrethrum shuts down the insect's nervous system. It breaks down in a few hours, leaving no trace and making it safe for humans and pets. However, to be safe, keep pets and children away from the plant and don't touch it without gloves until it breaks down.
- **Cinnamon:** It is more than just a tasty spice. Cinnamon oil prevents fungus and bacteria growth. It also has a strong scent that will prevent your pets from chewing on your orchids.
- **Neem Oil:** It repels insects with its astringent and antifungal properties. Neem oil is safe, light, and protects plants against aphids and spider mites.

Chemical Solutions

Pesticides

These are the most popular chemical solutions against pests. However, you should exercise caution since they contain harmful chemicals. Before using pesticides, you should always determine the kind of pest you're dealing with. Read and follow the instructions. When applying, wear a face mask and gloves, and wash your clothes after you finish. Open the windows to improve air circulation.

Pesticides don't just eliminate pests but protect from future infections but you will need to apply them regularly. However, you should be careful as they may damage delicate leaves.

Fungicides

Fungicides target fungi and prevent fungal diseases. They can also protect against scale, aphids, and other pests. Systemic and contact are the main types of fungicides.

Plants absorb systemic fungicides to protect them from the inside, while contact fungicides eliminate the fungus on the orchid's surface.

Read the instructions before using fungicides. Remember, they contain chemicals and can damage your orchid if you misuse or overuse them.

Orchid Diseases and How to Treat Them

Plants can suffer from other diseases that can affect their health and growth. Learning about these diseases and their treatments can help you save the plant from infections before it's too late.

Mosaic Virus

It is one of the most common orchid viruses and infects plants for various reasons, such as using contaminated tools like scissors to trim leaves or roots. Infections can easily spread if your plant pots are placed too close together.

Symptoms

- Light green or yellow leaves
- A mosaic pattern on the leaves.

Treatment

Viral infections can't be treated. Unfortunately, you will have to discard the plant. Prevent infections in other plants by using sterilized tools, isolate new plants from old ones, and avoid sap contact between plants.

Botrytis

Botrytis is a type of fungus that thrives in high humidity and spreads in places with poor ventilation. It mainly infects flowers but can also affect stems and leaves.

Symptoms

- Black or brown spots on flower petals.
- Gray mold on the plants

Treatment

Remove the sick flowers or they will infect the rest of the plant. Apply fungicides to prevent the botrytis from spreading. Read the label and follow the instructions. Examine the plant regularly, especially in winter, to ensure the infection doesn't return.

Anthracnose

Anthracnose is a fungal disease that can infect orchid leaves. You can easily recognize its symptoms because they appear on plant parts above the soil.

Symptoms

- Leaf tips turning brown
- Gray discoloration

Treatment

If your orchid becomes infected, place it in a different room to keep it away from healthy plants. Remove infected leaves and apply fungicide.

Anthracnose spreads in low light, high humidity, and low temperature. Prevent it from spreading and save the uninfected parts by creating an environment that protects against infection.

Fusarium Wilt

Fusarium wilt spreads in environments with warm weather and appropriate humidity, which are the ideal conditions for orchids. It attacks the orchid's vascular system, preventing nutrients and water from reaching the rest of the plant, which slows down its growth, leading to its eventual death.

Fusarium wilt's symptoms are subtle, making them hard to recognize.

Symptoms

- Slightly yellow leaves
- Slow growth
- Purple discoloration inside the stem

Treatment

If stems turn purple, the infection has spread, and you should discard the plant, or it will infect the rest. However, if fusarium wilt hasn't spread, cut the infected areas, sterilize the tools, and apply fungicides such as thiophanate methyl. Read the instructions before using.

While raising orchids is relatively easy, you can still run into problems. You can prevent these issues by creating a healthy environment for your plant with proper ventilation and keeping it away from harmful substances. Recognize symptoms of pests, fungus, and other diseases and treat them immediately.

Chapter 8: Orchid Propagation – Growing More Orchids from One

Do you know you can grow more flowers from just one orchid? With this simple process, you can grow as many orchids as you want. This chapter explains the technique of growing new orchids from keikis, the steps to divide orchids the right way, and cross-pollination and hybridization for advanced growers.

23. There's a process to help you understand orchid propagation. Source:

https://commons.wikimedia.org/wiki/File:Orchid_propagation_equipment_display_at_Kew_-_geograph.org.uk_-_1156298.jpg

How to Grow New Orchids from Keikis

Having an orchid and watching it grow is an amazing and fulfilling feeling. Once your new plant blooms and you see all the beautiful and colorful flowers, you will want to get another one.

Orchids are expensive, though. That doesn't mean you can't have more of your favorite flowers.

You can grow new orchids from keikis, a Hawaiian word meaning "The Little One." Orchid keikis are baby orchids that sprout from a mature plant. Species such as Dendrobium and Phalaenopsis can produce keikis. They are usually formed when an orchid is stressed or dying.

Baby orchids are created asexually, without pollination, so they look exactly like the original flower they sprouted from.

Keikis is usually grown on the stem of an older orchid. Once you recognize it, check your flower, which can be stressed or dying. The new flower will get its nutrients from the old one.

Some plant owners may not want to risk the well-being of their older flowers. You can simply cut off the keikis with sterilized scissors if you don't want it. Remove the flower's spikes to prevent the formation of more keikis.

Keep them if you want to have more orchids.

1. Leave the keikis on the older orchid until it has a couple of leaves, small shoots, and three inches of roots.

2. Cut two inches down the older orchid's spike to remove the keikis.
3. Put them in another pot with fresh soil. Make sure the roots are inserted deep in the soil.
4. Label the keikis's pot to tell it apart from the first one.
5. Mist it regularly and keep it away from sunlight. Baby flowers require higher humidity and less light.
6. Water the keikis and keep it hydrated.
7. Treat the cuts on the keikis and mother plant with cinnamon fungicide.

Dividing Orchids the Right Way

Dividing orchids is crucial to improve their health and growth and expand your plant collection. Take this step when they outgrow the pot or the potting medium deteriorates. The potting medium usually deteriorates every two years. You need to get a new one to prevent bacteria, fungi, and root rot and facilitate nutrient absorption.

You can divide your orchids when bulbs and new roots are formed or after flowering. Don't divide orchids when new blooms are forming, or the buds will fall off, and growth will slow down.

Instructions:
1. Clean and sterilize your pot with water and light bleach to remove fungus and bacteria.
2. Use alcohol to sterilize the scissors or the cutting tool you will use.

3. Remove the orchids from the pot. You can break it if necessary.
4. Discard old bark, rocks, or charcoal to expose the plants' roots.
5. Use the sterilized cutting tool and cut rotting bulbs and dead roots.
6. Cut the rhizome between the plants. Leave five pseudo buds for each new plant. Make large divisions for new plants.
7. Dip the roots in a rooting hormone such as Rootone to stimulate new growth.
8. Place your plants in a new pot with a new potting medium. Make sure it's fertilized.
9. Protect your newly divided plants with pins or wire to prevent the orchids from tipping over until new roots are established.
10. Water the plants.

Cross-Pollination and Hybridization for Advanced Growers

Hybridization is cross-pollinating two orchids to create a new variety for a specific fragrance, size, color, and flower form.

Instructions:
1. Clean and sterilize the surface area you will work on. Remove everything from the surface. Pollen is very small and you may lose track of it if your work area is cluttered.

2. Choose a tool with a sharp point to hold the pollen, such as a toothpick.
3. Hold the flower with one hand, hook the anther with the toothpick, and carefully place it on a clean surface.
4. Gently remove one pollen sac from the anther. It should stick to the toothpick. A sticky substance holds the pollen in its place, so it might snap back when you try to get it out. Keep trying gently until it attaches to the toothpick.
5. Place the pollen inside a different flower, not the one you took the pollen from.
6. Use the second flower's pollen to fertilize the first pollen.
7. Attach the pollen to the toothpick and move it to the column's opening, underneath the anther cap.
8. The pollen should now be inside the column. Push it as far as you can, but be gentle, or you may damage the plant.

Growing more orchids from your plant means having as many flowers as you want for free. If one of your flowers is dying, use the keikis to grow another identical one.

Flowers grow over the years, and your orchid may overgrow its pot. Dividing orchids can help you get rid of the unhealthy parts, rejuvenate the plant, and promote new growth and blooming flowers.

Cross-pollination allows you to create orchids with specific traits. However, this is a tricky process that is more fit for an experienced grower.

Chapter 9: Encouraging More Blooms and Longer-Lasting Flowers

This chapter has tips for you on encouraging more orchid blooms and making them last longer.

24. A few easy to follow tips will teach you how to keep your orchids blooming for longer. Source: https://www.pexels.com/photo/brown-orchid-flower-2923681/

Why Your Orchid Isn't Blooming and How to Fix It

Nothing is more frustrating for an orchid lover than waiting for your plant to bloom and seeing it refuse to grow those shapely flowers. You saw it flowering when you bought it, so why isn't it blooming again? Below are some reasons why this may be happening and how to fix them.

Not Enough Light

If your orchid doesn't get enough light, it won't have enough energy to produce flowers. Unfortunately, many new orchid owners underestimate how much light their plants need and end up with flowerless orchids. To verify whether this is the issue, check the leaves. It's time to move them somewhere brighter if they are dark green. Alternatively, you can use grow lights to encourage blooming.

Too Much Light

Your orchids may also refuse to flower if exposed to too much light. If their leaves are pale or have burn marks, move them to a slightly shaded place. Overexposure to light is likely suppressing the flowering phase. If you're using artificial light 24/7, this may also result in a lack of blooms. Ensure your orchids are exposed to the natural light/darkness cycle, whether in natural or artificial conditions.

Inadequate Night Temperature

Besides the lack of light, orchids also need cooler temperatures at night. If the night temperature of their environment isn't lower by 10 degrees than the daytime temperature, your orchid may not bloom. If you know when your orchid is supposed to flower, you can start acclimating it to warmer days and cooler nights about two weeks beforehand. It will reward you for providing its natural cue with beautiful flowers when the blooming season begins.

Lack of Proper Nutrition

Potting your orchids in an inorganic medium with only a small amount of fertilizer may also result in a lack of blooms. This common mistake stems from the belief that orchids don't need much fertilization. While this is true, too little nutrients in the soil means that the plant can't feed and create energy for itself. To resolve this, add some urea-free fertilizer to your orchid soil.

Lack of Room or Nutrients for Roots

Once the potting medium decays, the orchid's roots have no more nutrients or oxygen to use. Without these, your orchids won't flower. Likewise, they might refuse to bloom if they become rootbound, which happens when their roots run out of space in the soil. If the root system is tangled or creeping up to the top, and the plants become pale, it's time to repot them. This will likely resolve the issue, and your orchids will begin to bloom again. There is, however, a catch. After being transplanted, the plant can suffer repotting shock, which can also cause it to refuse blooming.

Too Much Water

While it's true that orchids love moist soil, if their roots become waterlogged, they won't flower. Plants can't absorb oxygen and nutrients when their roots become oversaturated with water. They will start to decay and reserve all their energy left over, leaving none for flower production. If you don't allow the soil to dry out at least partially between waterings, you're literally suffocating them, and you can't expect them to bloom. Check the roots. If they're brown, cut down on the watering and let the top of the soil dry before watering again.

Not Enough Water

Given their tropical origins, it's clear why underwatering would cause orchids to stop blooming. When you don't water them enough, these plants will take water from non-essential parts to sustain the essential ones. The first ones to lose water are the flowers/buds. Even if your orchids would have flowered otherwise and started to develop buds, they won't grow into flowers because the moisture is siphoned out. If you see buds turning yellow and fall off, your plant is in survival mode. You can fix it by watering it often. Keep in mind that watering frequency depends on the orchids and their environment. Some orchids need to be watered more frequently to bloom.

It's Not Time for It to Bloom

Contrary to popular belief, orchids don't always bloom in the same period you buy them (even if you purchased them full of flowers). Experienced growers know how to induce more frequent blooming, which can throw off beginners. You may be expecting your orchid to bloom when it isn't time yet. Some varieties bloom once a year but can be stimulated to flower more often. If you don't have a lot of experience, learn when your orchid is supposed to flower and focus on supporting it during that period. When you gain more experience, you can learn how to bring out additional blooming cycles of your orchids.

The Secrets to Getting Orchids to Rebloom

Many new owners fear that their orchids will never bloom again after they drop their flowers. If your plants have lost all of their flowers, they're likely in a vegetative state, which lasts 6-9 months. However, you can encourage them to shorten that period and rebloom naturally. The best time to do this is either spring or fall. During spring, your orchid will start its natural regrowth process, which, with adequate care, will result in flowering. The same effect can be achieved in the fall with the help of artificial lights and special care conditions.

How do you nudge your orchids to leave the vegetative state? By providing them with nutrients, which they can then convert into energy. Begin the intense feeding a few weeks after your plant has lost its last flower. Give them balanced houseplant or orchid-specific fertilizer every second week to supply them with nutrients without burning their roots.

Keeping proper hydration levels can also help kickstart reblooming. Lower watering frequency when you fertilize the orchids. Otherwise, stick to your regular schedule. Still, it's a good idea to monitor your plant's water saturation closely, especially if it's exposed to inconsistent weather or environmental conditions. For example, you should increase the watering frequency if the plant suddenly becomes exposed to higher temperatures and low humidity.

Cutting off the old spikes will also prompt growth because it signals to the plant that it's time to take in more nutrients to repair and rejuvenate the cut-off pieces. For this to happen, orchids must be kept at consistent temperatures (consistently warm for day/consistently cold for night).

While they enjoy warmth during the day, orchids don't like being close to direct heat sources. Avoid placing them near lights, air vents, heaters, etc. The air around these is particularly dry and can lead to dehydration.

Moving your orchids to a place with more favorable conditions may also encourage them to rebloom. For example, if your plant is exposed to too much light or hot temperatures and doesn't even have buds, moving it to a partially shaded, cooler place can help it flower sooner. Once your orchids bloom again, you can move them where they get a little more sunlight during the day but can enjoy cooler temperatures at night. Exposure to indirect sunlight is still recommended. It will continue blooming as long as you provide adequate care.

On the other hand, if your orchid has started growing new buds, moving it will not help. It can even cause the plant to stop the blooming phase and reenter the vegetative state.

Tricks to Make Blooms Last Longer

Orchids blossom on average for 6-8 weeks, but some species can be kept in bloom for up to 6 months. How long your plant's flower lasts depends on several factors. The first of these are watering practices. Not only will underwatering cause your orchids to refuse to bloom, but it can also make them drop their flowers faster. This is especially true for high humidity-dependent species that don't tolerate dry soil. If you want to avoid premature flower wilting, water your orchids as soon as you notice that the top layer of their soil is dry. If you resume watering in time, you can even save some slightly wilted flowers.

Tip: Keep your orchids in clear plastic pots. It will be easy to tell when they need watering and avoid droopy and dying flowers.

Another trick for making blooms last longer is always draining the excess water after irrigation. Water orchids in standing pots over the sink to ensure the excess water doesn't become trapped and cause waterlogging. This is why you shouldn't remove orchids from plastic pots, even if you place them in decorative ones. They can help prevent waterlogging, which could kill your flowers.

Most orchids bloom longer if watered with rainwater. However, if you don't have the opportunity to collect rainwater, bottled water will do just fine as long as it's fresh. Avoid using tap water as it's highly chlorinated. Let it sit for at least 24 hours before using it if you must use it. Always use room-temperature water. Too hot or too cold water can shock plants, making them drop their flowers prematurely.

Just like the lack of moisture in the soil, low humidity can also lead to flower loss. Remember, orchids thrive on humidity above 50%; for some, the optimal level is around 80-90%. Contrary to popular belief, misting isn't enough to keep orchids hydrated. A humidifier is the best way to help your orchids preserve their precious blooms for much longer.

Making sure your plant receives enough light during the day is another way to prolong its blooming period. They should be getting up to 14 hours of light exposure a day. Depending on the species, this can vary from partial exposure to sunlight (shade) or warm artificial lighting to exposure to filtered exposure to light. Get to know your plants and their light requirements.

If you live in an area where summers get scorching hot, you don't want your orchids to be exposed to direct sun (indoors or outdoors). Place them somewhere they won't get burned or dehydrated by the sun. Both of these factors will cause stress, and the first thing your orchids do when stressed is shrivel up and drop those beautiful blooms.

Tip: Expose them to the morning sun only, and make sure they will be protected by shade by midday.

The ideal temperature for making blooms last longer is around 60-85°F. Avoid exposing them to temperatures below 55°F and above 85°F. Even if not in direct sun, high temperatures are very harmful to your orchids and can make them drop their blooms. The same applies to low temperatures. If you're still learning the ropes and aren't versed in temperature tracking, keep your orchids inside, where it's much easier to control environmental factors.

If you're buying an orchid during cold weather, protect them when you're carrying them home. Stores keep their temperatures high to cater to plants' needs, and bringing orchids outside to the cold weather can be a massive shock to them. Even those few minutes between the store and your car can make them drop their flowers soon after you bring them home.

Invest in a leaf mister for liquid fertilization. Unlike many other plants, orchids can absorb nutrients from the fertilizer through their leaves, not just their roots. Misting them with an orchid-specific liquid fertilizer every two weeks will keep them in bloom longer.

Lastly, regularly inspect your orchids for pests, especially if you keep them outside. Some insects lay their eggs in orchid flowers to protect from the environment and predators. However, these eggs take nutrients and moisture from the flowers, causing them to shrivel up and die. Without intervention, all your orchid flowers will become infected and won't last long. Moreover, the insects can also release toxins that threaten the plants' health. Unhealthy plants seek to preserve energy, leading to dropping their flowers. Make sure to check the orchids from time to time. If you find any sign of pests, eliminate them and apply the necessary pest control measures. It's always better to sacrifice one or two flowers than to watch all of them lose their blooms.

Chapter 10: Creative Orchid Display and Styling Ideas

Adding beautiful blooming orchids to any decorative display can elevate its aesthetic appeal. This chapter offers tips on creating statement pieces for indoor or outdoor decoration and incorporating orchids into garden displays, terrariums, and more.

25. Learn the best ways to make your orchids stand out! Source: https://www.pexels.com/photo/a-person-holding-a-buddha-head-statue-beside-a-vase-of-pink-moth-orchids-7394396/

How to Create Stunning Orchid Displays Indoors

There are many ways to create orchid displays in indoor settings, including the ones listed below.

Combining Miniature Orchids

Take three or more miniature orchids in their pots and place them on a metal plate. Arranging several plants creates a very impactful statement piece for any table. You can add it to a coffee or dining table when you're expecting guests or on the kitchen table for a pop of fresh color when you aren't using the area.

Tip: Use orchids with matching colors. If you place the mini orchids in decorative pots, ensure the styles match.

Orchids in Bowl

You can also make a statement if you display a single potted orchid correctly. For example, placing it in a pedestal bowl would truly make it stand out. Find a bowl that matches the space's aesthetics, then pick and arrange the flowers according to the desired colors. Choose an orchid that's not too tall and has several blooming flowers.

Alternatively, you can place 3-5 small orchids in a bowl that isn't as tall (multiple smaller plants look better in horizontal arrangements). Place a bunched-up newspaper between the orchid pots in the bowl. That will stabilize them so they can stay as you arranged them.

Using one flower, you can incorporate additional decorations into the arrangements, including natural decor like preserved moss. This will give a natural and organic feel to the entire look.

You can display horizontal bowl arrangements on large tables, like the dining room table. Meanwhile, orchids on a pedestal will make excellent conversation pieces in foyers, living room tables, etc.

Orchid Centerpieces

Whether you want to display them in a bowl, plate, glass jar, or box, orchids make perfect centerpieces. Meant for larger tables for celebrations, orchid arrangements in the center of the table will elevate any event. It's one of the easiest ways to make flower centerpieces for special occasions. You can even enjoy these centerpieces for a long time afterward (or even gift them if you make more than one).

Place one or more orchids in the pots you want to use like the bowl arrangement. Arrange newspaper around the orchid pot and cover it with moss to finish the look. Use orchids with simple plastic pots for these. Or, if you want a more natural look, use clay pots.

Bathroom Display

Orchids are so versatile they can even upgrade the look of your bathroom. Naturally, you must choose plants that prefer low light conditions and high humidity. You can place them in a decorative pot on your bathroom shelves or windowsill, and they won't even be in your way. Or, add them to your guest bathroom, and your guests will have an elegant bathroom display to envy you for.

Tip: To complete the tranquil look, choose orchids with soft colors.

Play of Contrasts

One of the best ways to elevate the look of any design is to have contrast. If you have several orchid species or varieties with diverse flower shapes and colors, you can arrange them in a display for easy contrast.

If you have other plants, you can combine these with your orchids. For example, you can combine tall orchids with medium-height plants, regular orchids with plants that clash in color, or plants with different leaf colors and textures than the orchids, etc.

Tip: If you opt for this design, display it on an unadorned surface or against a simple background to avoid overcrowding.

A third option is to use orchids of the same or similar species, colors, and shapes and display them against a contrasting background. Place it in the living room or entrance area. Your guests won't be able to look at it without commenting.

Mounting Orchids on Wood and Hanging Arrangements

While potted orchids can make stunning display pieces, mounted orchids and other hanging arrangements can be even more versatile and effective. Mounted orchids can be hung or simply laid out on any flat surface, bowl, etc. These ornaments take less room, while those on flat surfaces are easier to mount.

One of the major benefits of mounted orchids is their longevity. When mounted, their roots are limited to growing within a small surface. There is no need to repot them, and they still last longer. It's best to mount your orchid when it starts growing new roots because these will help the plant attach to the mount. This is usually in the spring period for most orchid species.

Supplies for mounting:
- Hardwood mounts (white oak, dogwood, sassafras, mesquite, or highbush blueberry) or fruit tree months like citrus or cherry
- Tree fern slabs (optional as a mount instead of hardwood)
- Cork barks (optional as mounts instead of hardwood)
- Driftwood (optional as mounts instead of hardwood)
- Sphagnum moss or coconut fiber to wrap around the roots
- Wire
- Fishing line
- Wire snips
- Drill
- Needle-nose pliers
- Scissors
- A healthy orchid (Cattleya, Brassavola, Phalaenopsis, Angraecum, Tolumnia, and Vanda are the most recommended for mounting)

Instructions:
1. Remove the plant from the pot and release the soil around the roots. Be careful not to break them.
2. Soak the roots for 30 minutes in water. This will keep them hydrated and prepared to avoid mounting shock

(same as repotting shock). The water will also make them more flexible.

3. Remove damaged roots with clean scissors. You only want to use the healthiest part of the plant to increase its longevity.

4. Soak the moss or coconut fiber in water for 15-20 minutes. This will give the roots a headstart for water intake. Squeeze the excess water from the moss/fiber after soaking them.

5. If you're using a hardwood mount, you'll need to drill a hole to pass the fishing line and the wire.

6. Choose how you want to position your orchids.

7. Place the moss or coconut fiber on the mount and secure it with the fishing line.

8. Place and lay out the roots of the orchid on the mount. Gently spread them with your hand if necessary. Don't bend or force them in any direction, as this can break them.

9. Spread more moss or coconut fiber around the roots.

10. Use wire to secure the finishing layer of moss/fiber and orchid roots to the mount. Keep the wire tight but not as tight so it would dig into the roots.

You can create other hanging arrangements in decorative hanging pots besides orchids. These can add a pop of color to the balcony or any small space you want to decorate. Whichever hanging arrangement you choose, ensure it's easily accessible because you'll need to frequently water your orchids.

Terrariums, Decorative Containers, and Vertical Gardens

Terrariums can be the perfect solution to achieve more with your orchids than just an indoor flower display. They're a tiny piece of nature or a mini garden you can arrange to your liking.

How do you make a terrarium? You start by selecting the right container. It should be big enough to accommodate the orchid's roots even as it grows. See-through material is recommended to let in sunlight and elevate the visual appeal. The most recommended terrarium vessels are glass globes, jars, and bowls.

When it comes to the shape, you can choose what fits the aesthetic you're going for as long as it provides easy access to the plant. Lastly, make sure the container you use has drainage holes or slits at the bottom. Alternatively, you can place a layer of drainage material to prevent water retention and diseases.

Drainage can also be an issue with decorative containers used for simple displays (besides terrariums). Many lack drainage holes, so placing an absorbing material in them is an absolute must. For example, you can use activated charcoal, gravel, etc. Decorative containers come in all shapes and sizes, so you won't have a problem finding something that suits your aesthetics.

Always choose healthy orchids for terrariums and decorative displays. It's also a good idea to acclimate the ones meant for the terrarium. Place them somewhere they get less light and are exposed to higher humidity. Some of the most recommended species for terrariums are Phalaenopsis,

Paphiopedilum, and Miniature Oncidium. Before placing them, inspect the orchid for diseases. Remove them from their pot and trim damaged roots.

Prepare your terrarium by adding in a growing medium meant for orchids. These are formulated to provide nutrients, adequate airflow, and water drainage. Next, add decorative elements like driftwood, stones, branches, pebbles, and whatever else you want to use to bring your idea to life. For example, some like creating themed decorations, replicas of favorite landmarks, etc. You can then add the flowers, arranging them so each gets adequate light and airflow. Placing the shorter plants on the front and the taller ones on the back makes for an interesting display.

Besides terrariums and decorative containers, you can create natural displays by incorporating your orchids into a vertical garden. This is yet another solution for sprucing up urban areas where space is a luxury.

Instructions:
1. Prepare the orchids, rods (optional, to support larger orchids), the base, 2-inch thick pieces of felt, and a staple gun.
2. Remove the orchids from their pots and clean and cut the roots.
3. Place the plants where you want them in the vertical garden. Make sure they have adequate light.
4. If the orchids are larger, add a supporting rod next to them.
5. Secure the orchids and the supporting rods with the felt (staple the felt onto the base of the garden). Be sure not to catch the roots. Leave them free.

Vertical gardens are watered with hydroponic systems to ensure water gets to the roots of every plant. It keeps your stunning display alive and thriving.

Chapter 11: Advanced Orchid Care and Expert Tips

Now that you have learned how to grow and care for orchids, you are ready to tackle more advanced techniques. This chapter explores rare orchids and specialty species, DIY orchid care hacks that save time and money, and how to experiment with unconventional orchid care methods.

Growing Rare Orchids and Specialty Species

Orchids are among some of the most beautiful flowers worldwide. However, there are even more beautiful orchids that you probably haven't seen before. Among the diverse species of orchids are rare varieties that stand out due to their captivating colors and beauty.

Some rare orchids are demanding plants that aren't easy to grow. They don't tolerate mistakes like other species, so you should know their ideal growing conditions and determine whether you can provide a suitable environment for them. These specialty species need specific temperature, humidity, light, and watering requirements.

If you want your rare orchid to grow and thrive, you need to recreate its natural growing conditions at home. Their natural habitats are shady and humid, so you should create a similar environment by providing the plant with a planting medium that allows for proper drainage, such as sphagnum moss, perlite, and pine bark.

Rare orchids are similar to their counterparts in that they can't thrive under direct sunlight. Place the plant in a greenhouse, on an east-facing window, or on a shaded porch to promote optimal growth. Create a stable, ideal humidity and temperature.

Growing rare orchids can be easier once you familiarize yourself with their requirements and ideal environment.

Tampa Butterfly Orchid

26. Tampa butterfly orchid. Source: https://www.flickr.com/photos/dweickhoff/28268807391

This rare orchid stands out for its striking colors and stunning blooms. The Tampa Butterfly orchid is a protected species mainly found in Florida. In warm areas, it grows on trees and outdoors but is usually kept indoors in cooler regions. This orchid thrives in 50% humidity and bright indirect light. In the daylight, it requires temperatures between 65 and 85°F and 50 to 68°F at night.

Odontoglossum Orchid

27. Odontoglossum orchid. Source: https://commons.wikimedia.org/wiki/File:A_and_B_Larsen_orchids_-_Odontoglossum_grande_x_williamsianum_646-20.jpg

You may have never seen the Odontoglossum orchid before because it isn't easy to grow. However, experienced growers may be more familiar with it. Its captivating colors and shapes make it a popular house plant in cool areas. It is native to mountainous regions such as the Andes. In the daytime, it thrives in temperatures between 65 and 77°F and 50 to 60°F at night. It requires high humidity and filtered bright light.

Clamshell Orchid

28. Clamshell Orchid. Source: https://www.flickr.com/photos/berniedup/6776046663

The Clamshell orchid is famous for its unique clam-shaped flowers with petals resembling tentacles. It comes from South and Central America. You will rarely find it in the wild, but it is more common as a houseplant. This orchid thrives in indirect bright light. In the daytime, it requires temperatures between 70 to 80°F and 50 to 65°F at nighttime. It also needs high levels of humidity between 50 to 80%.

Zygopetalum Orchid

29. Zygopetalum orchid. Source: https://commons.wikimedia.org/wiki/File:A_and_B_Larsen_orchids_-_Zygopetalum_Titanic_Spritsig_DSCN4436.JPG

Zygopetalum orchid is the perfect household plant, thanks to its pleasant scent that will make your home smell nice. It also has an alluring form and colors, making it a great addition to your decor. You may not find this rare flower in gardens, but you can purchase one from a specialty grower. Zygopetalum orchid is an easygoing plant that is ideal for beginners. You will rarely experience any of the common orchid problems with this flower.

The Zygopetalum orchid requires moderate humidity between 50% and 70% and bright indirect light. It thrives in temperatures between 70 and 80°F during the day and 50 to 60°F at night.

Tulip Orchid

The Tulip orchid is also called "Swaddled baby orchid" because it looks like a swaddled baby. This is one of the most beautiful and unique flower formations you will ever see and is extremely popular among enthusiasts. However, the tulip orchid isn't easy to grow because it requires specific conditions. Greenhouses usually provide the ideal condition for this orchid.

You can still grow it at home, provided you create the right environment. It requires humidity between 60 to 70% and partial shade. In the daytime, temperatures must be 70 to 80°F and 55 to 65°F at nighttime.

Calanthe Orchid

30. Calanthe orchid. Source: https://commons.wikimedia.org/wiki/File:Calanthe_masuca_%27-

200601%27_(D.Don)_Lindl.,_Gen._Sp._Orchid._Pl._249_(1833)_(50299984382).jpg

Calanthe orchid, also known as "Christmas orchid," is native to Southeast Asia. It is easy to care for, making it the perfect choice for beginners. You can grow it in a garden or indoors. It thrives in humidity between 50 % and 70% and requires temperatures between 14°F tand84°F.

Monkey Orchid

The Monkey orchid, also called "Dracula simia," is a member of the Dracula genus that looks like a capuchin monkey. It has an unusual and interesting flower. This orchid isn't easy to care for, so it may not be suitable for beginners. However, you can try it if you like a challenge.

Dracula genus orchids don't like direct sunlight, hence the name. They thrive in full or partial shade and 80% or more humidity. You must mist them frequently and use a humidifier to keep them moist. They require temperatures of 60°F to 85°F and low temperatures at night. You should move them to a cooler room in the evening.

DIY Orchid Care Hacks That Save Time and Money

No plant owner wants to see their plant wither and die. You spend time and money on your orchid, and it can be frustrating to see all your hard work go in vain. Luckily, DIY care hacks can revive your plant and save you time and money.

For instance, if the soil doesn't meet all your orchid's nutritional needs, you can provide it with homemade fertilizers to boost it.

Banana Peel Homemade Fertilizer

The insides of banana peels can provide orchids with many nutrients such as tin, magnesium, and phosphorus. They can help your plant grow and prolong its life.

Instructions:

1. Peel two bananas.

2. Cover them with a glass of water and leave them overnight.
3. Place directly onto the soil.

Black Tea

Instructions:
1. Place two black tea bags in boiling water.
2. Let them sit for an hour.
3. Water the orchid with the tea.

Rice

Instructions:
1. Heat water in a large bowl.
2. Add a cup of rice and stir.
3. Leave for an hour to allow the starch to come out.
4. Water the plant with the rice water.

DIY Orchid Potting Mixes

Coconut Husk Chips Mix

Ingredients:
- Container with drainage holes
- Water
- Perlite
- Fine charcoal
- Coconut husk chips

Instructions:

1. Rinse the coconut chips.
2. Mix two parts of coconut chips with one part perlite and one part charcoal.
3. Add water and let the mix sit overnight.
4. Squeeze out excess water and add to the orchid mix.

Sphagnum Potting Mix

Ingredients:

- Aerolite
- Medium sponge rock
- Sphagnum moss

Instructions:

1. Measure nine scoops of sphagnum moss in a measuring utensil.
2. Add one scoop of aerolite and two scoops of medium sponge rock.
3. Mix with a ladle and add to the orchid mix.

Fine Potting Mix

Ingredients:

- Perlite
- Fine charcoal
- Fir bark
- Redwood bark
- Fine-grade coco chips

Instructions:

1. Use a measuring jar and add four parts of redwood bark, fine-grade coco chips, and fine fir bark in a container.
2. Add one part perlite and one part fine charcoal to the container.
3. Mix until it turns into an orchid potting mix, and add to the orchid mix.

Bark Potting Mix

Ingredients:

- Peat moss/ cocopeat
- Tree bark

Instructions:

1. Place one part of the tree bark in a container.
2. Add one-fifth part of the peat moss and mix.
3. Soak overnight and add to the orchid mix.

Experimenting with Unconventional Orchid Care Methods

Use these unconventional methods to care for your orchid.

Potting Ideas

Try these pot ideas to give your flowers a unique look and enhance your home's decor. You can use a ceramic pitcher, teapot, teacup, mug, or boot.

Propagate with Potatoes

Use this method to propagate orchids. It is popular among gardeners and orchid enthusiasts and involves using the stem's dormant eye or node part. Potatoes are filled with nutrients and vitamins to help the stem grow into a healthy plant. You can use this method to grow as many orchids as you want.

Instructions:

1. Cut a piece of stem with the dormant eye in the center. Use an orchid you love so the stem piece produces similar flowers.
2. Seal both ends with wax to prevent root rot.
3. Remove the triangular thin sheath on the eye.
4. To keep the stem piece moist, you can create a small transparent greenhouse from take-out containers, disposable cups, or bottles.
5. Fill the container with a layer of moss and bark and add the piece of stem.
6. Sprinkle with potato water until it feels damp, and cover the container.

Rare orchids are exquisite, with beautiful colors and unique shapes. Some are difficult to care for, while others are easygoing. However, if you can create a suitable environment for them, you can give it a go. You have learned enough about orchids by now to challenge yourself.

If your plant isn't getting enough nutrients or doesn't look healthy, try homemade fertilizers to improve its health.

Chapter 12: Final Takeaways and Orchid Success Tips

Mistakes are inevitable when growing orchids. This is normal, especially for beginners. However, you shouldn't let this discourage you. You can learn from your mistakes and avoid them in the future. This chapter provides tips to help you grow thriving orchids, explains the most common mistakes beginners make, and includes orchid resources and communities.

The Five Golden Rules for Thriving Orchids

You have learned a lot about orchid care. Understandably, this can be overwhelming. This part sums up the five most significant rules of thriving orchids. You can always return to them if your flower isn't growing properly.

Rule #1: Lighting

Orchids need lighting to thrive, grow, and produce blooming flowers. They should be placed away from direct sunlight to prevent discoloring and burns. However, some orchids may have different lighting needs, so read the plant's tag.

Rule #2: Watering

All plants need water to grow and thrive. However, you need to know when to water your orchid and when to wait. Check the planting medium. If it's wet, don't water it to prevent root rot. If it's dry, hydrate it right away using soaking techniques.

Generally, water your plant when the potting mix is slightly dry. Always water your orchid thoroughly. Allow excess water to drain to prevent root rot.

Rule #3: Temperature and Humidity

Keep the orchid in stable room temperatures between 60-80°F and humidity between 40-60%. Don't place your orchid near cooling or heating vents and drafts. You should also keep your home ventilated to allow for air circulation.

Rule #4: Repotting and Fertilizing

Choose the right fertilizer for your orchid. Read the ingredients to ensure it includes all the essential elements. It should contain macronutrients and micronutrients for optimal growth and maximum bloom. During the growth period, fertilize your orchid every two weeks and reduce fertilization during the dormant stage. You should also repot the plant every two years.

Rule #5: Check for Root Rot

Tackling issues early on can help you find treatments to save your orchid before it's too late. Take the plant out of the pot and examine it. Trim the unhealthy roots, sanitize the pot or get a new one, and place the plant in the new pot. Healthy roots are usually green and moist.

Top Ten Mistakes Beginners Should Avoid

Learning about some of the most common mistakes people make when growing orchids.

Mistake #1: Sun Exposure

It's common knowledge that plants love the sun and thrive in it. However, orchids are different. Most orchids are tropical plants and prefer mid to high humidity. Sun exposure can dry the water and burn the leaves. Ensure your plant gets bright but indirect sunlight for six hours daily.

Mistake #2: No Repotting

Some people think orchids can live in the same container their entire lives. However, leaving the plant in the same pot can cause root rot. Roots may also stick out of the container, preventing the plant from getting nutrients, which affects its growth and causes death. Repot orchids every two or three years.

Mistake #3: Unnecessary Pruning

Trimming unhealthy roots and yellow leaves is necessary to prevent infections and keep your plant healthy. Pruning for any other reason is unnecessary and can do more harm than good.

Mistake #4: Wrong Planting Medium

Most orchid species grow on trees. Household orchids don't require soil. They can survive and thrive in a planting mix made specifically for them. You can make it at home or purchase it. It should be a mix of 20% sphagnum moss and 80% fir bark.

Mistake #5: Poor Air Circulation

Orchids require high humidity levels to survive. Without enough moisture, their leaves and roots will become stressed, dry, wither, and die. Proper ventilation ensures optimal growth and protects your plant against bacterial and fungal infections.

Don't mist the flowers directly, or they will develop dark spots and wilt. Instead, place a humidity train under the plant, use a humidifier, or keep your home ventilated.

Mistake #6: Underwatering or Overwatering

Many beginners don't know how to water their plants and end up with dry plants as a result of underwatering or rot roots due to overwatering.

Mistake #7: Repotting When Blooming

You should never repot your orchids while in bloom, or you will damage your plant. They may go into shock and won't have enough resources to cope with this traumatic transition. Repot your orchid either before or after it blooms.

Mistake #8: Using the Wrong Pot

Use a pot that allows for airflow and drainage. Avoid pots that retain moisture, as they can damage the roots.

Mistake #9: Over Fertilization

Orchids require fertilizers for a prolonged and healthy life. However, like water, too much fertilization can harm your plant. To protect your orchids, use fertilizers made for them. Read the instructions on the package carefully.

Mistake #10: Not Examine the Plant Regularly

Orchids are sensitive plants that can easily get damaged and die. They can also suffer from issues like pests and root rot. Regular inspections will help you spot issues early on and deal with them before they damage your plants.

Where to Find More Orchid Resources and Communities

You can find many communities online filled with other orchid enthusiasts. You can bond over your shared interests, ask each other questions, and learn from your experiences. You can find these communities on Facebook or Reddit.

Expand your knowledge and go on websites that will provide more information.

- https://www.interflora.co.uk/page/flower-types/orchids
- https://www.aos.org/orchid-care
- https://www.usbg.gov/orchid-care-tips
- https://www.orchidweb.com/orchids
- https://www.rainforest-alliance.org/species/orchid/
- https://www.justaddiceorchids.com/
- https://www.orchid-tree.com/
- https://www.kew.org/read-and-watch/orchid-family-tree
- https://www.marthastewart.com/2124479/orchid-care-tips
- https://www.orchids.com/?srsltid=AfmBOoqEdE9m2xVSLynuhPDzgVcTy3ksx1bYlHU7mzrAG-iv9w67S9qO

Growing a healthy orchid isn't hard. Provide your plant with a suitable environment that caters to its needs. Keep it away from direct sunlight, don't let it dry, and provide the ideal temperature and humidity for your flower. Learning about your plant's needs will help you avoid mistakes that can hinder its growth.

Conclusion

Orchids are some of the most popular flowers worldwide, thanks to their beautiful colors, shapes, and fragrances. Caring for these plants isn't hard, but you must follow specific instructions to have blooming and healthy flowers that can add a unique ambiance to your home.

The book began by introducing orchids and providing basic information about these beautiful flowers. It explained their history, popularity, anatomy, growth cycle, and the difference between epiphytic and terrestrial orchids. It also debunked common myths about orchid care.

You learned about Phalaenopsis, Dendrobium, Oncidium, and other types of orchids that are perfect for beginners. Experienced growers also discovered more advanced types.

Orchids thrive in specific temperatures and humidity levels. You need to choose orchids based on your home environment or make adjustments to create the right conditions for them.

Choosing the right pot and learning how and when to repot your orchid will keep it alive and blooming for long periods.

Bad watering habits can damage your plants. You should recognize if your orchid is overwatered or underwatered and fix any problems arising from poor watering techniques.

If you grow a plant indoors, you should learn about its light requirements. Some plants thrive in direct sunlight, while others don't. Orchids prefer the shade. You must create the proper lighting setups for them and choose between natural and artificial lighting options.

Plants require many essential elements to survive and flourish. They will suffer from deficiency and die if they don't get enough nutrients. Read the label on the fertilizers to ensure they cater to your orchids' needs.

If you recognize issues such as pests, dehydration, root rot, or yellowing leaves, you should use the tips in the book to save your plant and take precautions to prevent future problems.

Key Takeaways:

- Orchids are some of the oldest flowers and have a rich and unique history.
- Choose the right orchid based on your experience level and home environment.
- You can choose the best pot for your plant's needs by learning about each type and its uses.
- While watering plants is vital, you can harm your orchid by overwatering or underwatering it.
- Proper lighting helps your plant grow and thrive.
- Choosing the right fertilizer can result in maximum blooms and prevent nutrient deficiency.
- Plants can suffer from pests, dehydration, and yellow leaves. Solving these issues can save your orchid's life.

- Orchids are beautiful plants that enhance your home's decor and add beautiful colors to a room.

Thank you for reading the book, and don't forget to leave a review!

References

Akin, C. (2022, October 30). 6 Stages In The Life Cycle of An Orchid - Orchid Resource Center. Orchidresourcecenter.com. https://orchidresourcecenter.com/6-stages-in-the-life-cycle-of-an-orchid/

C;aire. (2016, November 27). Anatomy of an Orchid. My Orchid Diary. https://myorchiddiary.wordpress.com/2016/11/27/anatomy-of-an-orchid/

hill, ed. (2024, January 16). The History of Orchids. Love Orchids. https://www.loveorchids.co.uk/blogs/home/the-history-of-orchids?srsltid=AfmBOopgSksn6q82dOegyl_tRnX7Adk5W2owaX9COAx2Qtw4VbstlnL4

Ice, J. A. (2015, November 10). 6 Reasons to Be Thankful for Your Orchid. Justaddiceorchids.com; Just Add Ice Orchards. https://www.justaddiceorchids.com/orchid-care-blog/6-reasons-to-be-thankful-for-your-orchid

Steve. (2024, December 12). 10 Myths About Orchid Care You Need To Stop Believing. Https://Freeplantscare.com/. https://freeplantscare.com/10-myths-about-orchid-care/

The History of an Orchid. (n.d.). Sites.millersville.edu. https://sites.millersville.edu/jasheeha/webDesign/websites/OOroot/history.html

THE MEANING AND SYMBOLISM OF ORCHID. (2023, June 21). Natural Orchids Boutique. https://naturalorchids.com/blog/the-meaning-and-symbolism-of-orchid/

Zhang, S., Yang, Y., Li, J., Qin, J., Zhang, W., Huang, W., & Hu, H. (2018). Physiological diversity of orchids. Plant Diversity, 40(4), 196–208. https://doi.org/10.1016/j.pld.2018.06.003

Epiphytes: Meaning, Characteristics, Adaptations, Examples. (2019, April 20). BYJUS. https://byjus.com/neet/epiphytes/

Anna. (2017, February 14). *25 Easiest to Grow Orchids: A Beginner's Guide*. Orchid Bliss. https://orchidbliss.com/house-happy-orchids/

Bourke, H. (2023, August 31). *How to Choose the Right Orchid for Your Home*. Bourkes Florist. https://bourkesflorist.com.au/blog/how-to-choose-the-right-orchid-for-your-home/?srsltid=AfmBOooV2VvfxOIOILyjbMunZnqkrw_18pjlqndaCrj5Ok9NxIvu8vng

inFeatures, M. G. published. (2024, April 16). *26 Different Types Of Orchids – With Pictures & Information*. Gardeningknowhow. https://www.gardeningknowhow.com/ornamental/flowers/orchids/different-types-of-orchids.htm

Myorchiddiary. (2017, February 8). *Choosing your first orchid – what to look for*. My Orchid Diary. https://myorchiddiary.wordpress.com/2017/02/08/choosing-your-first-orchid-what-to-look-for/

Orchids, J. A. I. (2024, August 15). *How to Select a Healthy Orchid from the Store*. Www.justaddiceorchids.com. https://www.justaddiceorchids.com/orchid-care-blog/how-to-select-a-healthy-orchid-from-the-store

Stephenson, H. (2025, January 21). *How to choose the right orchid for your home*. The Independent. https://www.independent.co.uk/life-style/water-bathrooms-peru-royal-botanic-gardens-kew-b2683324.html

Better-GroOrchidBlog. (2019). Choosing the Right Potting Mix. *Better-Gro*. https://www.better-gro.com/orchid-blogs/choosing-the-right-potting-mix

Holmes, K. (2019, October 23). *How to Choose the Right Pot for Your Orchid*. Martha Stewart. https://www.marthastewart.com/2219615/how-choose-right-orchid-pot

Just Add Ice. (2024a, June 13). *3 Telltale Signs It's Time to Repot Your Orchid*. Justaddiceorchids.com; Just Add Ice Orchards. https://www.justaddiceorchids.com/when-to-repot-your-orchid

Just Add Ice. (2024b, September 5). *The Best Potting Medium for Orchids*. Justaddiceorchids.com; Just Add Ice Orchards. https://www.justaddiceorchids.com/orchid-care-blog/choosing-the-best-orchid-pot-media

Plagron. (2024, September 25). *Plagron - High-Quality Growing Products for Successful Growing*. Plagron. https://plagron.com/en/hobby/grow-topics/repotting-plants-without-transplant-shock

Rhoades, H. (2021, June 19). *StackPath*. Www.gardeningknowhow.com. https://www.gardeningknowhow.com/plant-problems/environmental/learn-how-to-avoid-and-repair-transplant-shock-in-plants.htm

World, G. (2019). How to repot orchids. *BBC Gardeners World Magazine*. https://www.gardenersworld.com/how-to/grow-plants/how-to-repot-orchids/

AJ. (2020, December 8). OVER WATERED AND UNDER WATERED ORCHIDS - Orchid Den. Orchid Den - for All Your Orchid Needs. https://orchidden.com.au/over-watered-and-under-watered-orchids/

Akin, C. (2021, December 31). Overwatered Orchid Leaves | Symptoms & How to Fix. Orchid Resource Center. https://orchidresourcecenter.com/overwatered-orchid-leaves/

Anna. (2012, May 8). 4 Quick Steps to Increase Humidity and Add Airflow for Orchids. Orchid Bliss. https://orchidbliss.com/easy-ways-to-increase-humidity/

Craig. (2023, March 4). How to Rescue Overwatered Orchid with Root Rot And Yellow Leaves. Highland Moss. https://highlandmoss.com/how-to-rescue-overwatered-orchid-with-root-rot-and-yellow-leaves/

Estela. (2023, September 22). Starting in the Orchid world? The Woes and Wonders of Orchid Care. Atami. https://atami.com/blog/cultivation/starting-in-the-orchid-world-the-woes-and-wonders-of-orchid-care/

Grant, A., Draiss, A., & Griffiths, M. (2024, May 5). How Often To Water Orchids – The Definitive Guide. Gardeningknowhow; Gardening Know How. https://www.gardeningknowhow.com/ornamental/orchids/how-often-to-water-orchids

Hughes, M. (n.d.). Watering Orchids with Ice Cubes Is Really a Thing—Here's How to Do It. Bhg.com. https://www.bhg.com/gardening/houseplants/care/watering-orchids-with-ice-cubes/

Just. (2023, July 13). How Humidity Affects Your Orchid? | Just Add Ice. Justaddiceorchids.com; Just Add Ice Orchards. https://www.justaddiceorchids.com/orchid-care-blog/just-add-ice-orchid-blog/bid/98302/how-does-humidity-affect-my-orchid

Miles, M. (2024, March). Is My Orchid Underwatered? How to Treat Dry Orchid Roots. Maxandmilesplants.com; Just Add Ice Orchards. https://www.maxandmilesplants.com/blog/is-my-orchid-underwatered-how-to-treat-dry-orchid-roots

Orchid Watering | A Complete Guide. (2024, December 12). Justaddiceorchids.com; Just Add Ice Orchards. https://www.justaddiceorchids.com/orchid-care-blog/orchid-watering

Orchids: The all you need to know Flower Guide | Interflora. (2025). Interflora.co.uk. https://www.interflora.co.uk/page/flower-types/orchids

Research Guides: Orchid FAQs: Home. (2019). Nybg.org. https://libguides.nybg.org/orchidfaqs

Robinson, W. (2023, June 9). Orchid Care 101: How Often Should I Water My Orchid? Waldor Orchids . https://www.waldor.com/blogs/news/orchid-care-101-how-often-should-i-water-my-orchid

The Ice Cube Method - Orchid Care For Beginners. (2025). Love Orchids. https://www.loveorchids.co.uk/blogs/home/the-ice-cube-method?srsltid=AfmBOooKBfepqDjvvHRzB_sM12nW0P_QY-993eWRMva98uQ2Fw81guvZ

The Ultimate Guide to Orchids and Orchid Care. (2024). Ambius.com; The Rentokil Blog. https://www.ambius.com/resources/blog/plant-profile/the-ultimate-guide-to-orchids-and-orchid-care

VanZile, J. (n.d.). Learn Simple Tips for Watering Orchids and Common Mistakes to Avoid. The Spruce. https://www.thespruce.com/how-to-water-orchids-1902821

Wiley , D., & Neveln , V. (2018). Here's How Often to Water Orchids for Beautiful, Healthy Plants. Better Homes & Gardens. https://www.bhg.com/gardening/how-to-garden/how-to-water-orchids/

American Orchid Society. (2025). *Growing Orchids Under Lights - American Orchid Society*. Aos.org. https://www.aos.org/orchids/growing-orchids-under-lights

Barnett, T. (2021, November 21). *Orchid And Light: What Are Optimal Orchid Light Conditions*. Gardeningknowhow; Gardening Know How. https://www.gardeningknowhow.com/ornamental/flowers/orchids/orchid-light-requirements.htm

How to Give Your Orchids the Right Light and Watch Them Bloom. (2013, November 19). Orchid Bliss. https://orchidbliss.com/light/

Just Add Ice. (n.d.). *Seasonal Changes to Expect With Your Orchid*. https://www.justaddiceorchids.com/hs-fs/hub/52259/file-2164880279-pdf/docs/SeasonalChanges_Orchids.pdf?t=1460396394313

Ranges, T. (2025). *Central Vancouver Island Orchid Society*. Central Vancouver Island Orchid Society. https://www.cvios.org/temp-ranges

dora. (2019, December 6). What's Organic Fertilizer- Definition & Type | Dora Agri. Dora Agri-Tech. https://doraagri.com/what-is-organic-fertilizer-for-plants/

Dubaniewicz, K. (2021, February 19). Common nutrient deficiencies in plants - and how to fix them. Blog.bluelab.com. https://blog.bluelab.com/common-nutrient-deficiencies-in-plants#nitrogen-deficiency

Fabian Seed Farms. (2023, April 5). Understanding Liquid Fertilizers: Types, Application Methods, and Benefits. Fabian Seed Farms Inc. https://fabianseed.com/liquid-fertilizers-types-application-methods-and-benefits/

Fabian Seed Farms. (2024, February 2). Foliar Fertilizer : Elevate Your Plant Health In Alberta. Fabian Seed Farms Inc. https://fabianseed.com/foliar-fertilizer/

Robinson, L. (2024, September 4). Granular Fertilizer: Choosing the Right One | Verdesian. Verdesian Life Sciences. https://vlsci.com/blog/granulated-fertilizer/

Team Orchid-Tree. (2019, April 20). Why do orchids need fertilizer?. What are the nutrients required for orchids? Orchid-Tree. https://www.orchid-tree.com/blogs/fertilizing/why-do-orchids-need-fertilizer-what-are-the-nutrients-required-for-orchids?srsltid=AfmBOoqKIt9hX_Iz-upzvGUff2WY8of_CZ0i5R9pmagTmtXrfccvKJz4

VanZile , J. (2024). Learn How to Maintain Healthy Orchids With Proper Fertilization. The Spruce. https://www.thespruce.com/how-to-fertilize-indoor-orchids-1902815#toc-how-to-fertilize-orchids

4 Natural Ways to Insect and Fungus Proof Your Orchids. (2013, December 16). Justaddiceorchids.com; Just Add Ice Orchids. https://www.justaddiceorchids.com/orchid-care-blog/4-natural-ways-to-insect-and-fungus-proof-your-orchids

Akin, C. (2023, May 2). Orchid Pest Control |Controlling Common Pests. Orchid Resource Center. https://orchidresourcecenter.com/orchid-pest-control-controlling-common-pests/

Anna. (2017, December 15). Why Are My Orchid's Buds Falling Off? - Orchid Bliss. Orchid Bliss. https://orchidbliss.com/orchid-buds-falling-off/

Bud Blast - American Orchid Society. (2025). Aos.org. https://www.aos.org/orchid-care/orchid-pests-and-diseases/bud-blast

Gillette, B. (2023). How to Recover From Orchid Root Rot and Save Your Plant. The Spruce. https://www.thespruce.com/how-deal-with-orchid-root-rot-7090606

Griffiths , M. (2018, July 23). Orchid Buds Falling Off: How To Prevent Orchid Bud Blast. Gardeningknowhow. https://www.gardeningknowhow.com/ornamental/flowers/orchids/orchid-buds-dropping.htm

How to Fix Orchid Root Rot (Symptoms, Care, & More). (2020, December 11). Orchid Bliss. https://orchidbliss.com/how-to-fix-orchid-root-rot-symptoms-care-more/

Moulton, M. (2023, December 7). The 8 Most Common Orchid Diseases and How to Treat Them. Epic Gardening. https://www.epicgardening.com/orchid-diseases/

Vellon, N. (2023, November 26). Reviving Your Dehydrated Orchid: A Guide to Successful Recovery. La Foresta Orchids. https://www.laforestaorchids.com/blogs/news/reviving-your-dehydrated-orchid-a-guide-to-successful-recovery

Why Are My Orchid Leaves Turning Yellow? Reasons and Remedies. (2024). Gardenia. https://www.gardenia.net/guide/orchid-leaves-turning-yellow-reasons-remedies

Dividing Your Orchid. (2019, October 27). Better-Gro. https://www.better-gro.com/orchid-blogs/dividing-your-orchid

Gillette, B. (2023, December 4). Is Your Orchid Growing a Baby Orchid? Here's How to Plant It and Grow Another Orchid. The Spruce. https://www.thespruce.com/orchid-keiki-care-guide-8404533

How and when to divide perennials. (n.d.). Extension.umn.edu. https://extension.umn.edu/planting-and-growing-guides/dividing-perennials

Orchid Hybridization - Smithsonian Gardens. (2022, November 11). Smithsonian Gardens. https://gardens.si.edu/exhibitions/orchids-hidden-stories-of-groundbreaking-women/orchid-hybridization/

shadowolfdg. (2025). Guide to Pollinating Orchids — Steemit. Steemit.com; Steemit. https://steemit.com/nature/@shadowolfdg/guide-to-pollinating-orchids

What Is an Orchid Keiki & How Do I Care for It? (2020, February 1). Better-Gro. https://www.better-gro.com/orchid-blogs/what-is-an-orchid-keiki-how-do-i-care-for-it

Anna. (2017, February 14). *Learn How to ReBloom Orchids Step-by-Step - Orchid Bliss*. Orchid Bliss. https://orchidbliss.com/rebloom-orchids/

Di Lallo, Raffaele. (2022, November 2). *How Long Do Orchid Blooms Last + Tips to Last Longer*. Houseplant Care Tips. https://www.ohiotropics.com/2022/11/02/how-long-do-orchid-blooms-last/

Just Add Ice. (2024, September 19). *How Do You Get an Orchid to Rebloom?* Justaddiceorchids.com; Just Add Ice Orchards. https://www.justaddiceorchids.com/orchid-care-blog/when-do-orchids-rebloom

McIntosh, Jamie. (2024). *Discover Common Reasons Why an Orchid Won't Bloom and How to Fix Them*. The Spruce. https://www.thespruce.com/orchid-wont-bloom-1315978

ukhouseplants. (2025). *How to Achieve & Prolong Orchid Blooms*. Ukhouseplants. https://www.ukhouseplants.com/plants/how-to-achieve-prolong-orchid-blooms

Anna. (2018, June 5). *The Complete Guide to Mounted Orchids - Orchid Bliss*. Orchid Bliss. https://orchidbliss.com/mounted-orchids/

Hume, K. (2024, April 23). *Decorating with Orchids: Easy Orchid Display Ideas - Perfecting Places*. Perfecting Places. https://perfectingplaces.com/decorating-with-orchids-three-ways/

Kim, J. (2024, April 8). *DIY Orchid Terrarium Ideas for a Beautiful Indoor Garden*. Cute Farms. https://cutefarms.com/blogs/blog/orchid-terrarium-ideas?srsltid=AfmBOorxLjcO-hIjcoQ4zD_ek1IiJvRSXj2FbrHDn8yqexuJSUA4iFRV

Little Tree Garden Market. (2024, January 14). *Beginners' guide to interior design with orchids*. Little Tree Garden Market. https://www.littletreegardenmarket.ca/news/279/beginners-guide-to-interior-design-with-orchids

SingularGreen. (2022, January 20). *Orchids in Vertical Gardens: How to Plant*. SingularGreen. https://www.singulargreen.com/en/orchids-in-vertical-gardens/

Craft, R. (2024, April 8). The Unexpected Potato Hack That Makes Propagating Orchids A Breeze. House Digest. https://www.housedigest.com/1555580/propagate-indoor-orchid-potato-hack/

Griffiths, M., & Draiss, A. (2025, February 20). 8 Rare Orchids That Make Stunning Houseplants – Some Are Surprisingly Easy To Grow. Gardeningknowhow; Gardening Know How. https://www.gardeningknowhow.com/ornamental/orchids/rare-orchids

https://www.facebook.com/telegraficom. (2022, June 25). Homemade Orchid "Fertilizer": Three Simple Recipes That Will Revive Your Flower. Telegrafi. https://telegrafi.com/en/pleh-per-orkide-bere-ne-shtepi-tri-receta-te-thjeshta-qe-te-rikuperojne-lulen-tuaj/

Ice, J. A. (2015, November 17). 5 Unconventional Pot Ideas for Your Orchid. Justaddiceorchids.com; Just Add Ice Orchards. https://www.justaddiceorchids.com/orchid-care-blog/5-unconventional-pot-ideas-for-your-orchid

Rizvi, S. (2021, July 6). 4 DIY Orchid Potting Mix Recipes. Urban Plants™. https://urbanplants.co.in/blogs/news/4-diy-orchid-potting-mix-recipes?srsltid=AfmBOoqvP7D1JGNdJ3dMz8KkLpwu_xEsEn0SEsRBdrYs6Zgk UjvozZi9

Tremblay, C. (2024, April 4). The Secrets of Growing Rare Orchids: A Delicate Art to Discover. Serres Lavoie. https://serreslavoie.com/en/blogs/news/les-secrets-de-la-culture-des-orchidees-rares-un-art-delicat-a-decouvrir

BB Orchids team. (2024, December 19). 5 Things You Should Not Do With Orchids. Bborchids.com. https://www.bborchids.com/blog/common-problems-when-growing-orchids/

Chalmers, A. (2023). 10 Tips to Keep Your Orchid Thriving, According to an Expert Horticulturist. The Spruce. https://www.thespruce.com/orchid-growing-tips-7558944

Common Mistakes to Avoid when Growing Orchids – MG Orchids Online Store. (2025). Mgorchids.in. https://mgorchids.in/common-mistakes-to-avoid-when-growing-orchids/

G, A. (2023, October 10). Unlock the Secrets to Thriving Orchids. Be.green. https://be.green/en/blog/unlock-the-secrets-to-thriving-orchids?srsltid=AfmBOoqeTscy-FwnBr4ToJ54rOvIoZD9vTzf8NDfXSS1T2ADJ8wMurQT

Grant, A., & Draiss, A. (2024, March 2). 7 Orchid Care Mistakes To Avoid If You Want More Beautiful Flowers. Gardeningknowhow; Gardening Know How. https://www.gardeningknowhow.com/ornamental/orchids/7-orchid-care-mistakes-beginners-always-make

Strauss, M. (2023, January 26). 15 Common Mistakes to Avoid When Growing Orchids. Epic Gardening. https://www.epicgardening.com/orchid-mistakes/#Not_Inspecting_Regularly

Printed in Great Britain
by Amazon